R 1799 45 - 5-11 march 05

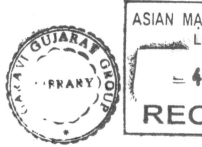

Brewing for Victory

Brewers, Beer and Pubs
in World War II

My Goodness — My GUINNESS

LOT OF BOTTLE: Guinness used their light-hearted advertising to good effect during the war, adapting their famous slogans to wartime themes as in this Gilroy poster from 1941 (*Guinness Archive*).

Brewing for Victory

Brewers, Beer and Pubs
in World War II

Brian Glover

The Lutterworth Press

Cambridge

The Lutterworth Press
P.O. Box 60
Cambridge
CB1 2NT

British Library Cataloguing in Publication Data:
A catalogue record is available from the British Library.

ISBN 0 7188 2928 X

Printed in Great Britain by
Hillman Printers (Frome) Ltd.

CONTENTS

LIST OF ILLUSTRATIONS

ACKNOWLEDGEMENTS

This is a story which was almost not told. I would like to thank the Brewers and Licensed Retailers Association for their financial support which made the publication of this book possible.

Many individual brewers and brewing companies also supplied information and inspiration, in particular Ken Thomas of the Courage Archive and Nicholas Redman of the Whitbread Archive. Thanks to them and to the Brewery History Society, especially Ian Peaty. I would also like to thank my brother, David, for help with the information on Sheffield.

The cover photograph shows American and British soldiers celebrating on VE-Day, and is reproduced with the kind permission of The Trustees of the Imperial War Museum.

ENEMY BEHIND THE LINES
Beer in the First World War

'Drink is doing us more damage in the war than all the German submarines put together,' declared Minister of Munitions David Lloyd George in 1915. 'We are fighting Germany, Austria and drink; and as far as I can see the greatest of these three deadly foes is drink.'

It was no idle comment. The powerful politician, who was to become Prime Minister in 1916, was one of two avowed teetotallers in the five-man war cabinet. Lloyd George believed beer was an evil influence. He was as determined to break the brewers' grip on Britain as he was to defeat Germany on the battlefield.

'This traffic, having sown destruction and death, must reap for itself a fruitful harvest of desolation and ruin.' He spoke like a pulpit preacher dedicated to his cause. A leader of Welsh nonconformism, he had supported complete prohibition in Wales since the 1880s. But Bills to introduce such measures had been repeatedly blocked in the House of Commons by what Lloyd George described as 'the brewers' ring which seems to govern England.' Now, in the emergency of war, he gained his revenge.

DORA, the Defence of the Realm Act of 1914, was a formidable piece of legislation with sweeping powers, which were repeatedly strengthened throughout the conflict. The licensed trade felt the full force of its measures.

In 1915 a Central Control Board (Liquor Traffic) was established to impose strict licensing hours in areas deemed militarily important. Eventually these covered virtually all heavily populated regions. Opening times were restricted to five-and-a-half hours a day. Pubs could only sell beer from 12–2.30pm at lunchtime and from 6–9pm in the evening on weekdays. On Saturdays the landlord had to put the towels over the pumps an hour earlier at 8pm. On Sunday drinkers barely had time to knock back a half. These were crushing changes. Previously customers had been used to being served from 5.30 in the morning until late at night.

Prices shot up as a huge burden of taxation was imposed on beer. The cost of a pint doubled from 2d to 4d between 1914 and 1916, later increasing to 5d before the Government imposed a measure of

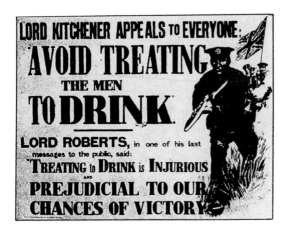

THE ENEMY WITHIN: Drink was regarded by the Government as a danger to the war effort in the First World War.

price control. At the same time the strength of beer was slashed, dropping like a stone from an average gravity of 1052 in 1914 to 1030 in 1918. Production was drastically cut back from over 37 million bulk barrels in 1913 to 19 million in 1917.

In some places where vital munition works were in operation like Carlisle, breweries were taken over and closed down, the pubs falling under State control. Lloyd George favoured the nationalisation of the whole brewing industry, which was seriously considered in 1915 and again in 1917.

The dry hand of the State even extended to slapping down the happy habit of buying your friends a drink. Treating was prohibited.

It was not just the harsh restrictions which alarmed the brewers – some were to be expected in war-time – as the atmosphere of official hostility. Beer was regarded as a danger, an intoxicating beverage which could undermine the war effort. The brewers were in the opposite trench, along with the enemy.

The industry knew they were not in favour – and fought back. DORA was depicted as a wicked witch, a gaunt and mean old lady snatching away John Bull's precious freedom. Many were convinced there was a conspiracy. One brewer from South Wales, George Westlake, blamed the new orders on 'fanatical teetotallers' who were using the war to push their 'fiendish propaganda for the purpose of wiping out the trade.'

This was not far from the mark as the temperance activists pursued their own agenda. One leader, Sir Thomas Whittaker, believed the war provided them with a great opportunity to strike 'whilst the overshadowing issues of the war are accustoming the people to restricted liberties.'

Their high point came in 1917 when the United States started to twist the Government's arm. Food Administrator Herbert Hoover issued veiled threats that an increase in vital American grain exports to Britain would be difficult to secure without an end to brewing in Britain.

The United States was moving rapidly towards total prohibition and expected Britain to follow. The Americans were climbing onto the moral high ground from where they could look down on their debauched allies, who were continuing to brew while the German submarines sank grain-carrying ships in the Atlantic.

The United States stopped brewing beer in December 1917, ostensibly because of the food shortage in Europe though more because of the overwhelming power of the teetotal lobby across the country. By the time national prohibition was introduced in January 1920 through the Volstead Enforcement Act, 33 of the 48 states had already adopted prohibition, covering more than two-thirds of the population.

The British cabinet considered the question carefully. It was dangerous to offend a powerful ally, but eventually the ministers drew back from taking the final measure because of fear of industrial unrest. In March 1917 Britain's Food Controller, Lord Davenport, had moved to meet the Americans, issuing an order limiting brewing to 28 per cent of its pre-war level, a mere 10 million standard barrels. This target figure was never reached. Ministers came to realise they had squeezed the public's pint too far. Sir George Cave, the Home Secretary, told the House of Commons in July 1917:

> The beer shortage is causing considerable unrest, and is interfering with the output of munitions and with the position of the country in this war. There is unrest, discontent, loss of time, loss of work and in some cases even strikes are threatened and indeed caused by the very fact that there is a shortage of beer.

Beer was no longer a problem. Shortage of beer was. Restrictions were relaxed and output rose to 23 million bulk barrels in 1918.

The Great War had given Britain's brewers a great fright. Talk of prohibition or nationalisation continued into the 1920s – but ironically the emergency measures taken during the war saved the industry from more drastic action.

When the Central Control Board was abolished in 1921, many of its restrictions were continued in the 1921 Licensing Act, notably the limitations on pub hours. Bars continued to close in the afternoon with last orders in the evening at 10.30pm or earlier. There was no return to all-day drinking.

Similarly the heavy duty on beer remained. This ensured prices never reverted to their pre-war level – and more significantly ale never regained its stupefying strength of 1914 when the average gravity had been 1052. In 1920 the average gravity was 1039 and by 1939 had barely edged upwards to 1040. The drunk, a familiar feature of Victorian and Edwardian Britain, staggered off the streets. Convictions for drunkenness in England and Wales fell by three-quarters from 188,877 in 1914 to 46,757 in 1937.

This new sober nation did hold some drawbacks for the brewing industry. The amount of beer drunk dropped so much it pushed the brewers into joint action. At the height of the Depression in 1933, consumption had collapsed to 17.7 million bulk barrels, lower than the worst year during the war and less than half the 1914 figure. In a bid to boost demand, the industry launched a 'Beer is Best' campaign with posters and adverts stressing the goodness in a glass.

Even the Carlisle State Brewery continued – and showed the way to the rest of the trade between the wars by pursuing a vigorous policy of building fewer but better pubs. Leading companies like Mitchell's & Butler's of Birmingham and Whitbread in London took great pride in their new, light, airy houses, offering such novelties as food and ladies' toilets. The number of pubs in England and Wales declined by more than 4,000 from 60,331 in 1918 to 56,173 in 1938.

When the war clouds gathered again in 1939, conditions were very different from what they had been 25 years before. One temperance supporter, Sir Harold Bellman, conceded:

Looking back over the lifetime of a generation, there has been an astonishing growth in general sobriety. . . . At the beginning of the present century the problem of alcoholism was menacing, both in extent and intensity; today, on any reasonable view, there has been a transformation which amounts almost to a social revolution.

The Brewers' Journal added in September 1939:

The last war accustomed the people to all kinds of restraints and restrictions. Some of them were proved by time to be good and they have been embodied in our national life. Others, when hostilities had ended, were seen for what they were – opportunist attempts to thrust on the masses the inclinations of the few.

In the present conflict the nation comes first and service

and devotion to its cause are paramount. But guard must be set at our gates lest the licensed trade becomes, as in the last war, the target of teetotal attacks guised under the cloak of patriotism.

The brewing industry had won most of the skirmishes between the wars, but now that full-blooded battle was joined again, it could not be sure that the Government would not buckle before the demands of its enemies.

ALLY ON THE HOME FRONT
The New Standing of Beer

When Hitler stormed into Poland, the war began. The temperance movement launched an all-out attack on alcohol. The dry campaigners scented victory. They were confident that in a national emergency, the Government would see booze as a threat and imprison this internal enemy behind roll after roll of barbed regulations, just as had happened in the First World War.

Almost before the first bullets had been fired, they shot out their manifesto under the title 'Alcohol – A Foe to Britain'. The National Temperance Federation declared war. It called on its three million members to wage 'earnest and unceasing national service in the conflict with alcohol.'

Lloyd George's warning in 1915 that 'drink is the most menacing of the nation's enemies' was used as a rallying cry. The teetotallers warned ministers that 'the national danger is too serious for official complacency.' They painted a lurid picture of beer and spirits sapping the nation's strength in its hour of need:

> The darkened streets, the consequent dangers of the roads, the uprooting of families from their homes, the gathering of our young manhood in camp and barracks, the strain and vigilance of thousands in the defence precautions, the increased demands on the munition makers, the general excitement and anxiety of the times – all these are only the earliest of the war's afflictions.
>
> In such a situation public houses packed nightly to suffocation are a blot on the nation's honour. We therefore proclaim that it is the duty of every good citizen to confront drink, the enemy of the country, with the example of his own self-discipline and determination to abstain while the war lasts. It is equally the duty of the Government to see that Britain's strength is not wasted nor her cause endangered by the lure of drink.

The Federation demanded the immediate introduction of the full First World War restrictions, and a few more besides:

1. Drinking hours shall be reduced to five-and-a-half per day

(with a break of two hours during the afternoon) to end not later than one hour after sunset, and in no case later than 9pm. On Sundays the total hours must not exceed four. In Wales drinking in clubs (as in public houses) shall not be permitted on Sundays.

2. Spirits shall not be sold anywhere on Friday night, Saturday or Sunday and, in defined districts, as in the last war, none shall be sold at any time.

3. The 'No Treating' order of the last war shall be reinstituted.

4. There shall be a further dilution of spirits and of beers.

5. Medicated wines to bear labels showing alcoholic content.

6. There shall be no canvassing for liquor orders and no advertisements calculated to induce the consumption of liquor.

7. It shall be a rule for air pilots, motor drivers and others engaged in any occupation wherein a high degree of neuro-muscular co-ordination is required, that no drink at all shall be consumed whilst on duty or for a prescribed number of hours before going on duty.

8. There shall be a progressive restriction of the national output of liquor through the regulation of the raw materials of the brewing, distilling and wine-making industries, and the diversion of land, labour and materials to the increase of the national food supply.

After issuing this long list of demands, Lady Astor in Parliament on 21 September, 1939, pressed the Home Secretary to introduce these measures at once in the interest of 'national safety'. She particularly wanted to see the reimposition of the No Treating order 'for the protection of men and women on duty in the defence services against hospitality by the public.'

Never mind the might of the German army, it was the chap at your elbow threatening to buy you a drink, who was the real enemy.

The Home Secretary, Sir John Anderson, refused to be stampeded into action. 'I am watching the situation carefully, but as yet I have no information to indicate that special measures are needed to check the consumption of alcohol.' He pointed out that pub opening hours in 1939 were 'very much shorter' than those existing before the First World War.

The dry campaigners were not deterred. The big guns were brought to the front-line. Early in November a letter appeared in *The Times* from the Temperance Council of the Christian Churches signed among others by the Archbishop of York and the Cardinal Archbishop of Westminster urging on the public 'the supreme necessity of self-restraint in the use of alcoholic liquors' during 'these grave and critical days.'

The more hard-line southern district of the Independent Order of Rechabites turned on the troops, passing a resolution calling on the Government 'to abolish the issue of the rum ration and the free distribution of beer at Christmas throughout His Majesty's Services.'

But their most effective tactic was to concentrate on the feared food shortage. The argument was that barley was being wasted in producing beer, when it could be fed to animals. Ernest Winterton, the former MP for Loughborough, summed up their position in a letter to the *Manchester Guardian* in November 1939, calling for an immediate reduction of liquor production by at least 50 per cent:

The Minister of Agriculture now announces that pig and poultry producers must expect a cut of at least one-third in the feeding stuffs available from abroad and that, with a much greater pig and poultry population than during the Great War, there will be short rations for many of them. This intimation warrants me in asking: When are the brewers – who monopolise so much shipping space by the importation of foreign barley – to be rationed too? Is it to be a case of beer before bacon or eggs? We have been scornful about 'Guns before Butter' (a German slogan). In our case, is it to be beer before both guns and butter?

This pigs before pints debate alarmed the brewers. The traditional demands of the temperance movement could be treated as the irrelevant ramblings of a spent force. *The Morning Advertiser*, the licensed trade's daily paper, dismissed the archbishops' letter to *The Times* as 'a venerable chestnut'. But the food issue could not be ignored. The threat of rationing was in the air.

Thus right from the outbreak of war the brewers went to great lengths to claim exceptional food value for beer. *The Brewers' Journal* of October 1939 claimed that a barrel of beer had the equivalent food value of the following: 10lbs of ribs of beef, 8lbs of shoulder of mutton, 4lbs of cheese, 20lbs of potatoes, 1lb of rump steak, 3lbs of rabbit, 3lbs of plaice, 8lbs of bread, 3lbs of butter, 6lbs of chicken and 19 eggs. 'We would emphasise that a standard barrel of beer has the food value of the WHOLE of the above food,' stressed the industry magazine. 'We have had these figures checked by a chartered accountant.'

Beer was no longer just a refreshing, enjoyable, social drink. In war-time it had to become a nourishing and sustaining beverage as well.

The claims were based on the findings of a committee of the Royal Society, set up by the Government in 1916 to investigate the food value of beer at a time when some ministers were flirting with the idea of total prohibition. With regard to alcohol in beer, the committee reported:

Accurate experiments have shown that alcohol if taken in moderate doses – up to the amount contained for example in one quart of beer – is very completely burnt in the human body, the proportion which remains unchanged being at the most some 5 per cent. This combustion of necessity liberates energy in the body . . . this energy need not be lost as waste heat but can be made to support the active functions of the body. This being so, a moderate quantity of alcohol may, if the conditions serve, actually take the place in nutrition of a dynamically equivalent amount of fat or of sugar.

And the argument did not end with the amount of calories a pint could provide. The brewers pointed out that alcohol acted as an aid to digestion, improving the absorption of other foodstuffs. While at a time when reliable water supplies might be disrupted or unavailable, it was claimed that the hops in beer supplied a vital antiseptic.

The Brewers' Journal was fond of quoting the late Professor Armstrong's statement that: 'Beer is the safest drink the world over.' This was backed up by the findings of Mr TK Walker of the Manchester College of Technology that: 'Weight for weight, the humulon or antiseptic agent in hops is 40 times as powerful as pure phenol or carbolic acid.' Mr Walker concluded: 'The more bitter the hops used in the making of beer, the stronger its antiseptic value is likely to be. . . . It is largely due to hops that, from the bacterial point of view, beer is the safest drink in the world.'

The Brewers' Journal in October 1939 listed the full qualities of beer, the wonderful beverage that 'stands in a class by itself':

1. Alcohol – a food in a form that requires no digestion.
2. Malt – protein in a most easily assimilative form.
3. Hops – a tonic bitter.
4. Sugar – a highly energising food.
5. Yeast – a vitalising and cleansing agent.
6. Mineral salts – needed for bone-building.

The value of the salts was especially emphasised. 'No other

beverage contains mineral salts and these in time of war are of high importance, particularly to men engaged in hard physical tasks which result in the loss of perspiration.' The magazine concluded: 'On all counts, therefore, as a war-time drink "Beer is Best", and the nation must see to it that it has a plentiful supply.'

The brewers were eager to ensure that ale was classed as a vital food rather than just an intoxicating drink. In the words of Dr Justus von Liebig, 'beer is liquid bread.' Viewed from that angle, it was more likely to avoid restrictions.

The Brewers' Journal called on the industry's 'Beer is Best' advertising campaign to ram home the point. The new message was that beer was not just best but very good for you. 'The public should be told in war time of the food value of beer and, moreover, of the enormous importance to the country of the by-products of beer.'

This was the brewers second line of defence. The malted barley used in brewing did not vanish completely into the beer. The spent grains from the mash tun were sold to farmers as an important cattle feed. The Royal Society report on brewing in 1916 had concluded

BEER IS BEST: The Brewers' Society had been promoting beer as a healthy drink for a fit nation throughout the 1930s. This poster dates from 1934.

that '2lbs of brewers' dried grains (when fed to milch-cows) yield 1.34lb of milk' and that when fed to horses the grains are worth 'pound for pound with oats.'

The industry was also able to highlight the valuable vitamins supplied by the use of brewers' yeast in products like Marmite which had grown considerably in popularity between the wars. 'White bread is notoriously lacking in vitamin B. Brewers' yeast, prepared in the form of "meat extracts" to which the public have become accustomed, will remedy this defect,' said *The Brewers' Journal*.

The magazine even suggested that British troops should carry dried brewers' yeast with them in their combat kit, after learning that Finland's heroic soldiers, fighting against the might of the vast Russian forces, had included dried brewers' yeast as part of their iron rations. *The Brewers Journal* concluded:

At the time when the need for an adequate food supply for the nation is being stressed, these facts are of the highest importance to agriculturists and to those whose duty it is to concern themselves with the food of the nation in time of war.

The words were wasted. These arguments barely swayed the Government and had little effect on the public. But both ministers and munition workers valued beer for other reasons. The man in the public bar believed it was the best drink at the end of a hard day. The Government knew a relaxing pint or three was vital in maintaining morale.

The industry quickly recognised this and returned to emphasising beer's more traditional and obvious qualities. 'Beer is the possessor of many virtues to which other foods have no claim,' declared *The Brewers' Journal*, going on to quote a number of eminent authorities:

'Beer is a soothing beverage,' said the late Professor Dixon in his presidential address to the British Medical Association.

'All factors which promote happiness promote health, and as beer promotes happiness it promotes health,' said Dr J L W Thudichum.

'Beer gives a more cheerful aspect to life and helps us through the difficult times in which we are forced to live. A bottle of beer in the evening is for many the only path to true and refreshing sleep,' said a further medical man.

'In times such as these, people need some liquid sunshine,' added another.

The public did not need these testimonials. Many looked forward to a drop of beer. Their worry was that the Government might introduce rationing. The industry was also deeply concerned.

WHAT THE SITUATION DEMANDS

1. WHEEL *for putting shoulder to*
2. SOCKS *for pulling up*
3. STONE *for not leaving unturned*
4. BRASS TACKS *for getting down to*
5. TRUMP CARD *for playing*
6. BOLD FACE *for putting on it*
7. BELT *for tightening*
8. GUINNESS *for strength*

STOUT ART: Guinness caught the wartime mood with this backs-to-the-wall poster from 1942 extolling 'Guinness for Strength.'

The words of J R Clynes, MP, a former Food Controller and Home Secretary, must have come as a welcome clarion call, when he wrote in the *Daily Sketch* on 6 January, 1940, under the headline 'Hands off Britain's beer':

> I have heard a number of rumours that beer rationing is being considered. A shortage of maize stocks, accentuated by reduced imports, has caused hundreds of farmers to feed barley to their cattle in these winter months. This has shortened barley supplies, and rationing of beer is therefore said to be under consideration. I am flatly against it.
>
> I know the need of the man engaged in heavy war industries for his occasional glass of beer; and he does not want to get out a ration book every time. To men in heavy industries beer is food, and necessary food at that.
>
> During the last war when I was at the Food Ministry, we had a hard fight to keep beer free of interference. . . . But I opposed it then as I will oppose it now. To the working man beer is food, drink and recreation.

The forces supporting prohibition and interference will

muster all their strength in an attack on beer. But the grain situation is not nearly so acute now as it was last time. . . . Hitler's submarines cannot threaten our country's beer – it will only be those in Britain itself who do not approve of workmen drinking beer who will try to banish it.'

To keep our factories humming and their workmen contented and healthy, it will be of the first importance to avoid creating a grievance among men who are working today harder than ever before.

One paragraph in this feature would have struck an alarm bell with the Government: 'I believe that any effort to ration beer would produce grave unrest among the workmen who are the backbone of Britain's industrial war effort.' It echoed a warning from the First World War, when the Home Secretary told Parliament in July 1917, that 'the beer shortage is causing serious unrest and is interfering with the output of munitions and with the position of the country in this war.'

The Government was well aware of the importance of the public's pint and in February 1940, the Minister of Food, Lord Woolton, appointed a leading industry figure, Hugh Paul, to act as his technical adviser on brewing. At the same time a Brewing Advisory Committee was formed comprising the top brewery bosses of the day led by the politically astute Sydney Nevile of Whitbread, who was also Chairman of the Brewers' Society.

In the First World War the brewers had been the outcasts, the black sheep, the enemy within. In the Second World War they came in from the cold, being officially embraced as an important part of the Government's war effort.

In May 1940 the Minister of Food, Lord Woolton, declared that he had no intention of stopping or cutting back the brewing of beer. The annual amount allowed was fixed at the barrelage produced in the 12 months to the end of 30 September, 1939. Shortage of brewing materials might mean its strength would decline, but as far as possible the barrels would continue to roll.

'If we are to keep up anything like approaching the normal life of the country, beer should continue to be in supply, even though it may be beer of a rather weaker variety than the connoisseurs would like,' said Lord Woolton. 'It is the business of the Government not only to maintain the life but the morale of the country.'

Drunkenness was not a major problem any more. 'We are in the fortunate position of having a temperate nation,' said Lord Woolton.

Be careful
what you say
+ where you
say it!

CARELESS TALK
COSTS LIVES

KEEP QUIET: Some temperance campaigners implied that pubs were riddled with enemy agents. But Government posters like this one had already warned against careless talk.

Later he added in the House of Lords, to loud cheers: 'There are many people who believe that a glass of beer is not doing anybody any harm.'

The teetotallers had lost the argument. They were furious. Some resorted to language last heard in the First World War. Dr Chevasse, the new Bishop of Rochester, told his first diocesan conference in June 1940: 'Alcohol we should regard as a fifth column, the enemy within our gates, sabotaging armament output, sapping morale and responsible for physical unfitness by inflaming passions.'

The Rev. W C MacDonald, at a temperance lunch in Edinburgh, echoed Lloyd George when he declared: 'Today we are facing three enemies – Germany, Italy and drink, and it is no exaggeration to say the worst is drink.' He added:

People are talking about invasion, but we should not trouble about that. No great empire has ever fallen because of an attack

DIG FOR ~~VICTORY~~ *PLENTY*

GUINNESS for STRENGTH

GROWING CONCERN:
Guinness posters were so
successful during the war that
this one was adopted by the
Government to encourage
people to get growing
(*Guinness Archive*).

from outside. History has proved that. Countries only went
down because they became decadent, morally corrupt, and
their strength was sapped by drink and all the other evils
that came in its train.

The National Temperance Federation lobbied MPs with a series
of questions:

Are you aware that the production of beer in war-time has
been fixed at the standard of that for 1939 – the highest for
ten years? . . . Can you justify the calling back of men to the
land from other needed services if the additional grain they
produce is malted, fermented and destroyed as a food by the
brewers?

The Conservative MP for Blackburn, Sir W Smiles, tried another
tactic to get a ban on treating, asking the Home Secretary on 4 June,
1940:

Whether he is aware that the treating of our soldiers, sailors
and airmen by strangers in public bars leads to conversation
and information which may often be of great use to the enemy;
and whether he will consider making such treating illegal?

With the German army having overrun the Continent and British troops limping back from Dunkirk, the front page of *Alliance News* proclaimed: 'The country has now become a besieged fortress. It is therefore imperative that the conservation of the nation's food supply should be regarded as a paramount consideration. Vested interests must at last yield to public pressure.'

Leaflets were produced by the National Temperance Federation demanding beer rationing and the return of the Liquor Control Board from the First World War. 'It is sheer hypocrisy to urge the people to "save food" and to "dig for victory" whilst vast quantities of valuable food supplies continue to be destroyed in brewing and distilling.'

But they were now the voices on the outside. The Minister of Agriculture, R S Hudson, in the House of Commons on 9 July, 1940, denounced the propaganda methods of the Federation as 'most discreditable.'

Oxford MP Quintin Hogg bluntly told his local dry lobby that they 'must clearly understand that the national emergency is not a moment to introduce temperance propaganda under the cloak of national necessity. Beer is the innocent pleasure of many millions, especially among those who bear the brunt today.'

Churchmen also raised their glasses. The Rector of Brampton, Rev. H J Sillitoe, told a licensed trade rally in Chesterfield in May 1940, that beer is 'God's good gift – a real asset to the social life of the nation.' The *Church Times* on 23 August, 1940, declared that: 'In war time, even more than in peace, man needs his cakes and ale. . . . Beer is part of the Englishman's diet. It cheers and heartens. It is the accompaniment of simple friendliness.'

Even the Royal Family acknowledged ale's new social standing. In the First World War King George V signed the pledge at the instigation of Lord Kitchener. In the Second World War, when Britain stood alone against the might of Germany in August 1940, King George VI stood in a cornfield in Dorset surrounded by schoolboys who were helping with the harvest. Glasses were filled and the toast was: 'To a speedy victory.' The *Daily Mail* reported: 'The boys had ginger beer and lemonade. The King preferred a glass of beer.'

So did the Government and the majority of the British people. And the favourite place to drink it was in the pub.

BLOCKHOUSE ON THE HOME FRONT
The Vital Role of the Pub

'The lights are going out all over Europe,' was the famous phrase which ushered in the First World War. In 1939 the lights went out two days before war was declared, with a black-out imposed on 1 September.

For pubs, which had always tried to stand out as bright as a boozer's nose in the evening shadows, this meant curtains for their glowing windows. Tapes were placed round the bright cracks, while bulbs near entrance doors were painted blue or removed altogether.

For customers it meant stumbling out into the dark, and trying to avoid dimly lit cars and lorries on the pitch-black roads. Accidents soared. And the gloom was not only on the streets.

Jack Showers who ran **The Stanhope** at Rodley, near Leeds, a pub famous for its live entertainment, recalled the first night of war in his book *Welcome Inn*:

There was a peculiar atmosphere abroad that night, and our band played half-heartedly to an audience that had ears tuned to the sound of the aero-engine rather than sweet music – death was in the air and his dark mantle had already penetrated deep into the minds of men. The whole place seemed unreal and I had a grim feeling that we were a crowd of marionettes about to dance to a deadly tune.

I could stand it no longer and, what was worse, I was sure that my patrons felt the same way, so I went up to the band leader and asked him to change the tune. I remembered the stirring war songs from the First World War and suggested that he should play 'Keep The Home Fires Burning', 'Tipperary' and so forth.

Reaction was electric for everyone sang lustily and the singing relieved the awful pressure. We all sang 'We Don't Want To Lose You, But We Think You Ought To Go', and I had a feeling that I was guilty of egging on the young men sitting around me . . .

In the dark days of the black-out, with cinemas and other public places of entertainment closed, the pub came into its own as a haven

BRIGHT IDEA: Shortly after the black out descended on London, Watney's introduced these clever stickers in the windows of their pubs.

of companionship and relaxation from the strains of war – once folk had got used to venturing out into the murky streets. Philip Boddington of Boddingtons' Breweries of Manchester told his first war-time AGM that the black-out had blanked out much of their business 'as was proved by the difference in trade noticed on light nights when there was a good moon.'

But the warm welcome of the pub in those chilling times proved impossible to resist. The MP, A P Herbert, summed up its value early in the conflict:

In these days, it seems to me, the British pub, the people's club, has justified its existence as perhaps it never did before. For it has been the one human corner, a centre not of beer but bonhomie; the one place where after dark the collective heart of the nation could be seen and felt, beating resolute and strong.

The attitude had changed from the days when most 'respectable' people looked down their noses at the common pub. The Rev. W F Geike-Cobb of St Ethelburga's in Bishopsgate, London, declared in a letter to the Press in October 1939:

Inns, from being the mere drinking shops of 25 years ago, have become social centres where rest, recreation and food for all are provided and where drunkenness is practically unknown. It would be neither fair nor sensible to discourage soldiers and citizens from visiting these decent places and thus to drive them to unpleasant, unsupervised haunts of the type that flourished during the last war as a result of some heavy-handed measures against inns.

Another cleric, the Rev. Edgar Rogers, the Dean of Bocking in Essex, elevated the pub even further, saying in January 1940: 'After the church, the public house ought to be the most sacred spot in town or village; and after the public house, the school.'

When Britain's expeditionary force narrowly escaped Hitler's marauding army in June 1940, beer consumption shot up, and not just because of the thirst of the returning troops. As the survey organisation Mass Observation observed: 'There was more to talk about than usual and the pub is above all a place where people can get together and talk to one another in groups.'

Rupert Croft-Cooke summed up the importance of the pub, as all ears were anxiously tuned to the latest news bulletins on the wireless. He had been travelling through the front-line counties of Kent and Sussex by horse-drawn caravan, and spent most of his evenings in public bars. In an article under the headline: 'A blockhouse on the home front' in the *Grimsby Evening Telegraph* on 15 July, 1940, he wrote:

The inn has become, since September, a thing of far greater significance than perhaps it has ever been . . .

The war has meant something more than a new and absorbing topic of conversation in the inn, something more than the absence on service of the younger customers whose faces were seen here nightly a year ago, something more than the presence of uniforms and the increased cost of beer and tobacco. It has meant, in almost every inn I know, a drawing closer together, a subtle, not easily perceptible, but quite definite new comradeship among men who are not soldiers and are not likely to be wanted as soldiers.

The news bulletins seem to have loosed tongues which have been silent on certain topics for 20 years, and to have revived a spirit of good fellowship, of being in the same boat, which in the years of peace lay dormant.

There are those who don't approve of pubs and inns and who are trying to take advantage of the war and close them down, or at least curtail the hours in which men may meet and talk and drink a glass of beer. The inn fulfils a useful function in time of peace. In time of war, it fulfils a more useful function still. It brings people together in a spirit of companionship and cements the common purpose. The inn is a blockhouse on the home front.

Pubs particularly took young men, away from home to fight the war, to their hearts. They became instant celebrities. Jack Showers recalled interviewing a bomber crew before his enthralled customers at **The Stanhope**:

I interviewed the whole crew in front of the mike and I can still sense the hush, even as I write, as the packed house heard them tell at first hand of how they had run into an electrical storm while over Germany and had the horror of seeing the 'kite' immediately in front of them struck; it exploded with the full bomb load on board. This novel news caught the imagination of the newspapers who featured it in their early morning editions the next day.

Naturally they were lionised that night, and I could see that it would be quite out of the question for them to return to base before morning, so we accommodated the eight of them. From that night on our place became the 'Target for Tonight' with these happy-minded heroes who visited us with regularity every 48 hours: in fact we adopted them as our pet bomber crew, for they all loved my wife who was a real mother to them. Many a happy night did those same boys spend with us, and many a grey dawn saw them depart, perhaps never to return; and we would silently watch and wonder.

The thing we had dreaded so long did come to pass, for one dark night the door opened and only one of that crew came in. Breathlessly we watched and waited, fearing the worst, for they had always followed one another in quickly. The story, however, was clearly written in the poor boy's eyes and, with a break in his voice, he told us that he had been sick and had not gone on the last flight. . . .

The value of the pub was even recognised by authorities which had previously been hostile. Birmingham Licensing Justices between the wars had pursued a vigorous campaign of closing pubs wherever possible. Now this policy was put on ice.

On 7 June, 1940, the threatened licence of an Ansells' house, **The Vine** in Ruston Street, was renewed after the brewery's solicitor had shown that **The Vine** was the only convenient pub where workers from two nearby factories 'engaged in essential war production' could 'obtain a glass of beer with their luncheon.' If it was closed, the solicitor argued, the workers would have gone further afield and there would have been a tremendous crush in other pubs 'which was the sort of congestion the Chief Constable was working to prevent.'

Not all, of course, approved. Temperance campaigners viewed pubs as the dens of the devil. Even before war had been declared, Wilfred Roberts MP, on 4 July, 1939, had asked the Secretary of State for War whether arrangements were being made to set up milk bars in the new military camps. Otherwise he feared the young men called up for training would troop off to the pub. Lady Astor asked the Secretary of State whether he realised how many women were terrified about sending their sons to camp on account of drink?

The teetotallers wanted pub opening hours severely cut back, particularly an earlier closing time in the evening during the black-out. Some authorities obliged. Glasgow magistrates closed houses at 8pm early in September 1939, though this precipitate action was quickly reversed.

Of immediate concern to the brewers on the outbreak of war was the sudden requisitioning of many hotels in supposedly safe areas by the Government, and the evacuation of people from threatened locations, depriving local pubs of much of their custom. Though when the bombs failed to fall in the first months many returned to their old haunts.

Of equal concern to both Government and brewers was the vexed question of pub cellars. In the event of an air-raid were they the proper place to protect the public? The general view was that cellars were not suitable in ordinary circumstances owing to the stocks of liquor and glass stored there. 'Where public houses are to be used as shelters it is highly desirable that stocks should be partitioned off so as to be inaccessible,' warned *The Brewers' Journal* in September 1939. That way awkward issues could be avoided. Such as would a drink direct from a cellar cask at 11.30pm be an offence or an acceptable way of steadying the nerves? And how would you ever get the customers out?

Instead of bombs, licensees in the first months of the war were hit by a steady salvo of regulations. A memorandum from the Home Office on 27 October, 1939, delved into pub cellars. Having recognised that during an air-raid 'an attempt to drive all customers out of premises would not only be contrary to the public interest, but would often be ineffective or impossible,' the Home Office came up with three recommendations for pubs when the siren sounded:

1. No more customers should be admitted.

2. Customers living or working within easy distance should be advised to leave at once for their homes or places of business.

3. For the remaining customers full use should be made of any suitable cellar accommodation.

The Government was also worried about the growing number of 'bottle parties'. These had first appeared in the 1930s. They were supposed to be private functions and so avoided the licensing regulations, serving drink into the small hours. In fact the 'guests' were any members of the public prepared to pay an entrance fee to the 'host' and high prices for the drinks once inside: 'It was all a ridiculous subterfuge,' fumed *The Brewers' Journal* in March 1940.

> At the present time, there are scores of them, often in basement rooms in office buildings . . . dangerous in an emergency for people who gather there, overcrowded and free from supervision. As many as 300 people crowd into a small space, drinking and dancing or watching cabaret now, since the war, almost certain to include nude women.

The brewing industry was angered by these unauthorised events which escaped all the regulations restricting pubs. They were even more annoyed by the Government's response. During the war these 'parties', usually open from 10pm until 6am, were packed with soldiers and sailors home on leave looking for a good time. In order to provide some alternative late-night entertainment, the authorities in London experimented with allowing restaurants, particularly Lyons' Corner Houses, to stay open until 2am, serving drinks without a meal. However the trial on two successive Saturdays in April 1940 was not a success. The Brewers Journal reported in June 1940:

> The experiment was doomed to be a failure for many causes, one of which is that a Corner House is hardly the place that people would select to spend a night out. Another is that the facilities offered were seized upon by the civilian denizens of Whitechapel whose custom is to flood the West End at weekends, and these people sat at the tables in the Corner House in such quantities that hardly any servicemen could be accommodated . . . and in that time ordered one drink apiece, so that the experiment was a dead loss to the proprietors. . . . The experiment deserved to be a failure since it was grossly unfair to the public houses in the neighbourhood which under the law were forced to close their doors.

Another Government initiative which dismayed the brewers was Lord Woolton's establishment of over 1,000 British Restaurants. These provided good, cheap meals in areas badly affected by the war. But many private caterers, including pubs and hotels, resented the unfair competition since the Government-backed British Restaurants could obtain ample supplies of meat at a time when many other restaurants were rationed. And as they were staffed by volunteers, their overheads were low.

The brewers believed pubs could help shoulder the burden of feeding the public, but during the war most licensees struggled to obtain sufficient food. Gravesend publicans were even warned that

HOME FROM HOME:
Many pubs became wartime
havens for unexpected
groups of people. When the
BBC Variety Department
was evacuated to Bangor in
North Wales during the
London Blitz, **The Vaults**
became the local for many
radio stars.

it was illegal to sell biscuits to a customer – to give to his dog in the
bar. Expanding pub grub beyond a pie, a pint and a pickled egg had
to wait until rationing disappeared.

One particularly awkward problem which bothered the bureau-
crats was the question of officers and men. Could they drink in the
same bar? The Minister of War, taking time out from conducting the
conflict, even found it necessary in class-ridden Britain to issue an
order stating that there was no official objection to officers and men
taking meals or refreshment together. Previously, landlords had been
expected to refuse to serve 'other ranks' if an officer happened to be
in the bar enjoying a glass at the time.

The War Office felt obliged to march in after 'Officers Only' notices
appeared in hotels near military bases. Many of the new recruits
were outraged and a flurry of letters hit the Press. The authorities
responded by stating: 'The War Office deprecates the posting of
notices in hotels or public houses reserving bars for officers only.
There is no authority for this.'

But not all local commanders kept to the spirit of this statement.
The Brewers' Journal revealed in February 1940 that: 'At Epping, for
example, two public houses patronised by the RAF have had to ban
the sale of drinks to all men below commissioned rank in certain
portions of the premises.' In these pubs the saloon was reserved for

officers. Landlords had little option but to agree. If they refused to bow to these demands, then the whole pub was placed 'out of bounds' to service personnel.

The problem was still causing disquiet in 1942, as shown by a spate of letters in the *News Chronicle*. Specific complaints were made about an 'Officers and Gentlemen Only Served' notice in a Gloucester hotel and the more ingenious 'Officers must show their official passes before entering' sign in a large hotel in Warwickshire. A sergeant pilot in North Wales flew into a rage because the dining rooms of his two local pubs had been placed out of bounds to him.

Such privileged treatment was resented in the people's war. It was especially disliked in what had become the heart of the communal war effort – the pub. Even visiting celebrities now stepped inside, as the licensed trade's paper, *The Morning Advertiser*, reported early in 1941:

Wendell Willkie [a leading politician who had opposed Roosevelt for the Presidency] threw convention to the winds when he left his Park Lane hotel and went to London's old Shepherd Market in the heart of Mayfair, walked into **Ye Olde Chesterfield**, ordered a pint of beer, and played a game of darts with a builder's labourer.

He was almost unrecognised as he entered the public house. One customer said, 'I took him for a Yankee boxer myself.'

Mr Willkie lifted his glass and drank to a party of soldiers, gathered round the bar, who were passing through London on their way home on leave. 'Have a beer on me, boys,' said the big laughing American, and in a moment every glass in the house was raised with the cry, 'Best wishes to you, sir.' Mr Willkie replied, 'I drink to you, lads.'

At the invitation of the licensee, Harry Phillips, Mr Willkie went behind the bar and pulled himself a pint of beer. 'This is where we get one on the house, boys,' he said. Mr Phillips told him, 'You did it very well, sir. How much a week do you want?'

Mr Willkie played darts in the public bar with Albert Phillips, a builder's labourer of Acton. He exclaimed: 'Look out boys. This is where you get shot.' He threw a good dart but was no match for his well-trained opponent.

After the game, the licensee performed a little ceremony that went straight to Mr Willkie's heart. Producing a half-bottle of 1929 champagne, Mr Phillips said: 'I was going to keep this for Armistice Day, but you are as good as an Armistice Day to us, and we will open this bottle together.' The American and the licensee put aside their beer and toasted each other in champagne.

Lunch-time customers kept Mr Willkie busy signing his autograph. The old market place rang with cheers as he drove away with the comment, 'Oh boy, that was fine.'

He had just enjoyed the magic of the pub for the first time. And the experience was spreading. As Captain A J Dyer, leader of London's licensees, said in an article in *The Star* newspaper early in 1942: 'In many districts, particularly those that have experienced raids, people who would never have dreamed of leaving their homes for a pub in the evenings, now come regularly to share the cheerful companionship.'

The war was also breaking down another taboo – that respectable women never went to the pub. A letter to the *Monthly Bulletin*, a newsletter dedicated to improving the pub, from a woman in the rural wilds of Essex, revealed the sea change that was going on at her village local, **The Bull**:

It began when East End mothers and daughters were evacuated. They went into the public houses as a matter of course. Perhaps the pub was the only place where there was a bit of fun. They were followed by the younger women of the village. Our cook went to **The Bull**, to the horror of her parents. Indeed, many village parents were horrified. The wives and sweethearts of the RAF have followed their men stationed amongst us; and there is the Women's Land Army.

The Bull was a quiet, sleepy (and rather unsuccessful) place in the old days. Now it's a regular village cafe – a bit noisy sometimes, but innocent enough – with dancing and a Channel Island refugee, a considerable performer, at the piano. Is this a bad thing, a sign of decadence? I don't think so. It means that the pub is changing its character, probably for the better. Women will in the long run ensure a higher standard.

The Brewers' Journal of April 1942 proudly proclaimed that the pub had become:

The meeting place where fellow men and women are to be found, and where for a brief space in a tiring day body and mind can be rested and refitted to face the arduous tasks of the morrow. And war-time, with its shifting scene of dark days and disappointments, estrangements and new ways of life

REST AND RECREATION: The pub provided a much-needed place to unwind during years of stress. Regulars could meet their friends and talk about the war over a game of dominoes.

and work, intensifies the need for these human comings together, and makes the pub a place of respite and reconciliation.

The *Journal* even pondered on the changing name of the pub: We wonder whether it has been noticed that the licensed house has been given a different appellation, varying with the times and with public feeling towards it. The turn of the century found it often termed the 'drink shop' or the 'gin palace'; in 1910 the cold term 'public house' was most usually employed. With the 'reformed house' period that followed in 1920 onwards, the 'inn' came into vogue. The 1930s found the 'pub', written just like that, in common parlance. . . . Now it is 'the local' – a neighbourly, part-of-us phrase that today finds increasing use on the wireless and in the Press.

The breaking down of old social conventions and the opening up of the pub to a much wider range of customers, did have one worrying result for the brewers. Under-age drinkers started to creep in. Young people, often catapulted into better-paid jobs because of the war, suddenly had money to burn and started to push on the bar door. The issue began to eat up column inches in the Press late in 1943.

The Bishop of Chelmsford in November called for an 8pm curfew for girls under 18 years old. The Archdeacon of Dudley moved that

OFFICIALLY APPROVED: A London ARP warden checks that the cellar beneath **The Norfolk Arms** in Islington is all clear before approving its use as an air-raid shelter. The three vaults could house over 200 people (*Courage Archive*).

the 'No Treating' order be reintroduced to counter the problem. The Archbishop of Canterbury, Dr Temple, agreed, saying that 'often those who were treated were unused to any kind of alcohol and did not know what its effects might be.'

The Home Secretary, Herbert Morrison, was asked in December to reintroduce the 'No Treating' order 'as one means to reduce the evil of excessive drinking among young people.' He refused. The alarmed trade quickly distributed notices to pubs warning against under-age drinking.

Even cinema-goers found the welcoming pub glowing at them from the big screen. Under the title 'Free House', a Ministry of Information film showed several sailors from different nations drinking in the bar of a pub. Each man tells why he left his own country to fight the Nazis. Beer flows freely. A British sailor enters and says that after the war they must share the wealth of the world, like they are sharing this barrel of beer. The glasses are refilled and everyone drinks to the future.

The local was attracting other strange visitors. In its revitalised role as the community's social centre, it was interesting academics.

Sociologist Dr J MacAlister Brew, writing in *The Times Educational Supplement* early in 1942, told her up-market readers her findings after visiting 100 pubs in 100 nights. This dedication to duty was in order to discover why young people went to the pub.

These young people do not go to the licensed house to drink.
They go there, as their forefathers did before them, to sit and talk and be sociable; to exchange news; and they drink to ease the process of so much talk in so close an atmosphere.

The bar not only provided welcome refreshment and relaxation in the dark days of fear, it was also the centre of a remarkable fund-raising movement. Altogether over 10,000 war savings groups were established in licensed premises, with astonishing amounts collected. One London suburban house raised £3,400 during War Weapons Week alone.

The Government was keenly aware how well placed the licensed trade was to raise money. One brewery company had already established 300 National Savings Associations in its houses in the first months of the conflict. Licensees were used to collecting money, having organised slate clubs, loan clubs and Christmas clubs for many years during the Depression. Now they were asked to supply their customers with 6d savings stamps along with their ale.

A special savings committee was established under Frank Whitbread early in 1940 to organise the brewing industry's effort. Off-licence shops as well as pubs were involved, besides workers groups in breweries and maltings. Over 100,000 posters were distributed depicting a civilian drinking his pint of beer accompanied by a soldier, sailor and airman above the caption 'Help your Pals. Join our Savings Group'. Each pub in the scheme carried a savings stamp sticker in its window proclaiming 'This is a War Savings House'. During special events like Warships Week streamers and banners were hung outside prominent pubs.

Some landlords used their own initiative, organising savings competitions between their saloon and public bar regulars. One self-sacrificing licensee put up a notice urging his customers not to treat him more than once a night – and invest what they saved in stamps. In Birmingham the savings scheme was linked to a bowls competition, raising £54,000 in 1941. Slogans like 'Lend to Defend' became familiar at the bar with the result that thousands of spare shillings were sucked into supporting the drive for armaments.

As the conflict continued, fund-raising became more ingenious. In November 1942, the brewing industry launched the 'Tank'ard

PULLING TOGETHER:
Over 10,000 war savings
groups were set up in pubs.

When there's a big job of work to be done it's a British
instinct to " lend a hand." Today Britain is faced with the
biggest job of work in all history — to defeat the evil forces of
Nazidom once and for all — and in the shortest possible time.

All together now!

We can't all fight with weapons in our hands but *everyone* — men, women and children, too — can give direct, continuous and personal help by saving as much as they can every week and lending it to the Nation.

JOIN A SAVINGS GROUP
Here's the simplest method — join a War Savings Group (or help to form one in your workshop, office or school). Your weekly savings will, all put together, make up a great

and ever-growing volume of money to back up our fighting forces with ample supplies and equipment.

And remember, too, all the time you are putting by this money you are saving for your own and your children's future.

• • •

Apply to your local Savings Committee, The National Savings Commissioner for your Region, or to the National Savings Committee, London, S.W.1.

SAVE to WIN the WAR

SAVINGS CERTIFICATES : DEFENCE BONDS : POST OFFICE AND TRUSTEE SAVINGS BANK

Fund' with the object of raising enough money to pay for a battalion of tanks. Britain's pubs were again to be the collecting boxes. Each house received a poster – showing a cowering Hitler in a tankard and the slogan 'Stamp on the Blighter'. The object was for customers to obliterate his hated face by buying stamps to stick on the poster. It took 200 6d stamps to cover up Hitler, and in June 1943, a cheque for £25,000 was handed over to the Treasury, with a further £8,000 for the Tank Regiment.

In 1944 it was the turn of the 'Salute the Soldier' campaign, with posters showing an inn sign in the centre on which to write the name of the pub, with space round the edge for customers to fix photographs and letters about regulars serving in the forces. London alone aimed to raise £165,000.

But the brewing industry was already supporting the colossal cost of the war against the Nazi dictator in another way – through escalating taxation on the price of a pint.

TAKE-OFF: Breweries organised their own fund-raising initiatives. Here landlords hand over a cheque for the Spitfire Fund run by George's Brewery of Bristol (*Courage Archive*).

NATION'S LIQUID ASSET
Beer Duty fills the War Chest

A Cockney walked into a bar after one year of the war and, plonking a sixpence on the counter, said: 'Pint o' mild an' bitter and 'arf ounce o' shag.' Then he paused, gazed down at the sixpence, and sighed: 'Strewf, I'm livin' in the past again.'

The war changed the relationship between the pint and the pocket beyond recognition. It also altered the relationship between the Government and the brewing industry. Beer duty funded the fighting.

The taxation on a tipple was increased three times in the first year, first doubling the basic duty from 24s a barrel to 48s at the start of the conflict in September 1939, then increasing to 65s in April 1940 and then shooting up again to 81s in July 1940. The combination of these three rises meant beer was now taxed at a rate 22 times greater than in 1914. These were the first changes since 1933 when duty had been reduced because Snowden's punitive budget of 1931 had led to a massive drop in consumption.

The brewers held their breath. While they knew they could not complain too loudly about helping to meet the cost of the war, they feared the worst. Each increase added a penny on a pint. Such a substantial hike in peace time would have seriously dented demand. Yet to everyone's surprise customers carried on drinking, swallowing the steep price rises – which saw the cost of a pint of mild leap from around 5d to 8d – with barely a grumble.

'The buoyancy of the beer output . . . has been remarkable, and is proof, if proof were needed, that British beer firmly maintains its position as the national beverage of the British people,' commented the Brewers' Society's Annual Report for 1940.

The only effect of the much higher prices appeared to be a certain amount of 'drinking down' where customers switched to cheaper beers and so accelerated the increased production of lower-gravity brews. Some also transferred their loyalties from the more expensive saloons to the public bars, helping to break down the old class barriers. *The Brewers' Journal* welcomed this new spirit of comradeship in adversity, even if it cost the trade higher profits.

It is surprising how much less of an outsider the other fellow is after a conversation over a glass of beer. And the incidence of the beer duty which puts into the mind of the man to go into the public bar to take his glass of beer at the same price as he paid a month or two ago in the bar parlour is likely to further this good fellowship, whatever repercussions it may have on the pocket of the licensee.

The sharp tax rises also left the brewers no room in which to add their own price increase – even though their costs had surged dramatically. Some brewers felt this patriotic sacrifice on their part was not being recognised. After the first war budget, Sir G L Courthope, chairman of Ind Coope & Allsopp of Burton, pointed out at the end of 1939:

Practically everything we require for production and distribution has increased in cost. Barley and malt have risen steeply. Hops have risen by an average of 10s a hundredweight. Brewing sugar has practically doubled in price. Fuel, petrol, casks, bottles and cases are all up, while wages have risen considerably and will probably rise further.

Yet not a farthing of this had been passed on to the customer.

At least the drinker received due recognition from the *Daily Sketch* newspaper in a lengthy editorial under the title: 'Patriot with a beer glass' on 27 April, 1940, following the second beer-bashing budget.

A few days observation since Sir John Simon opened his budget has established one fact which is always astonishing when we have a new revelation of it . . . it is the happy stoicism of the beer drinker under all assaults. He it is whom all Chancellors of the Exchequer elect as their first victim whenever they find themselves in a tight corner. So it was in 1914 in the first war budget, when Mr Lloyd George, explaining his new impost, said something to the effect that he knew the noble community which it affected would take it in good part. That noble community did . . . It obviously does not resent the additional tax as an injustice. It is happy enough to contribute what it can.

And there is a good reason for that. A good deal of the enduring life of our community has been built up round the places in which the noble community holds its meetings. Here, with talk and song and good comradeship, with darts and shove-ha'penny and devil-among-the-tailors, the spirit has been maintained which makes our people go into war as friends who know and trust one another. Waterloo was not only won on the playing fields of Eton. The tap room of **The Red Cow** had a good deal to do with it as well.

So let us give the noble community its due for patience and good humour. Not all of us drink beer . . . but even those of us who do not, ought to lift a glass of something, even if it should only be barley water, to the beer drinker who pays his taxes with so little complaint.

One teetotaller was even moved to express solidarity with his beer-drinking brethren. 'Aquarius' wrote to the *Western Mail* in Cardiff:

While I am profoundly convinced that those who indulge in intoxicating drinks are grievously mistaken, I am nevertheless compelled to realise that they are shouldering a very heavy proportion of the financial burden imposed upon us by the war.

If only therefore as a thank offering for the blessings of temperance, I feel that total abstainers in all parts of Great Britain should be only too pleased to contribute to a special fund for the purchase of Spitfires. I am enclosing £1 for the Spitfire Fund, and hope my fellow total abstainers will follow suit.

The brewers public protest was reserved for the way cider dodged the burden, receiving complete immunity from taxation. The rival alcoholic drinks industry had enjoyed this preferential treatment since 1923. 'The injustice of this discrimination in favour of cider is widely felt throughout the licensed trade,' said the Brewers' Society. Some companies feared cider – at half the price of beer – would sweep their products off the bar. A letter in the *National Guardian* from a Scotsman while on a visit to Yeovil in Somerset in the summer of 1940 demonstrated the value-for-money attraction of the apple drink:

The evening of the day we arrived here I went out with some of the boys to sample the cider. Drawn specially from the wood, and costing 3 d per pint, it tasted rather bitter and sourish, but I soon acquired the taste. I had 1s 2d worth. Anyhow there were no bad effects the following morning except for a sourish dry taste on the roof of my mouth. It is a cheap drink for fellows who haven't much to spend.

The brewers real reward came where it mattered – in the esteem of the Government. Even that arch temperance advocate Lloyd George had to admit when Chancellor during the First World War that drinking beer was vital for raising revenue. The words must have stuck at the back of his dry throat, but he forced them out: 'Every half-pint that a man drinks, he will be contributing to the carrying on of the war.'

The important role of beer in bankrolling the barricades (the three rises in duty in the first year of war meant beer raised a massive £150 million) meant that the Government was now prepared to defend the brewers against their critics. When the Scottish teetotal movement protested against the 'destruction' of food in brewing and distilling, Robert Boothby, the Parliamentary Secretary to the Ministry of Food, replied in strong terms in the summer of 1940:

It is not always remembered by the advocates of greater restriction that beer contributes very heavily indeed to the war effort in taxation and that, having regard to the already very low gravity of present-day beer, it would be impracticable to make any further marked saving in the use of materials used for brewing unless it were proposed to impose a most drastic restriction on the consumption of beer with corresponding loss of revenue to the Exchequer – a loss which would have to be made good by heavy taxation in other directions.

The brewers sealed their new relationship with the Government by donating the newspaper and magazine advertising space reserved for their 'Beer is Best' campaign to the Ministry of Information in June 1940. Individual brewers like Whitbread also handed over their poster sites. The move was widely applauded. It was also wisely appreciated. *The Brewers' Journal* commented:

The unanimous decision of the Council of the Brewers' Society to take this action means that brewers, as it were, have left their flank unsupported against the attacks of those who are using the war to press home teetotal propaganda. But the trade believes that both the Minister of Food and the Minister of Supply fully realise the part which a reasonable beer supply can play in encouraging the morale and well-being of workers who are putting their last ounce into the effort to equip the country's forces.

The space was used by a grateful Government to provide practical advice for the public in a popular series of newspaper notices on the theme 'What do I do . . . ?' Subjects covered included: 'What do I do if my home is made uninhabitable by a bomb?' or 'What do I do to keep my Anderson shelter healthy in winter?' Many people cut out and kept the useful articles, provoking a cartoon in *Punch* showing a sentry challenging a passer-by clutching his cuttings. 'Halt! Who goes there?' 'Half-a-minute, while I look up the "What do I do".'

Early in 1941 the Brewers' Society reprinted these articles in booklet form. The Minister of Information, Duff Cooper, thanked

What do I do...

if I am

challenged

by a sentry?

When I hear the words "Halt! Who goes there?" I stop *at once*. I answer: "Friend!" and wait until the sentry calls "Advance, and be recognised!" Then, and not till then, I step forward and show my identity card (which I always carry with me). If I am with other people each of us steps forward *one at a time*. Even if I'm in my own district, where I think I'm pretty well known, I still do exactly the same. These are serious times and if I treat the matter as a joke, I run the risk of being shot.

Cut this out — and keep it!

Issued by The Ministry of Information Space presented to the Nation by The Brewers' Society

WHAT DO I DO? One of the many 'What do I do' notices issued by the Government using the advertising space provided by Britain's brewers (left). This one prompted a *Punch* cartoon (below) showing a soldier demanding 'Halt! Who goes there?' To which the passer-by clutching his cuttings replies, 'Half a minute while I look up the "What do I do" '.

the society in a foreword 'for the help and support which they have given and are still to give in this way.' The minister appreciated 'the liberal and national outlook which has been characteristic of the society in these hard seasons of war.'

The rout of the teetotallers was complete. All the temperance movement could do was complain that the Government had accepted a bribe. But this did not mean the industry could escape further duty increases as the length and cost of the war escalated. The first three tax rises had staggered many. What shocked them even more was the way drinkers absorbed these heavy blows. Even the Government had budgeted for a drop in demand. After a respite of 20 months, the Chancellor followed up his early raids on the drinks cabinet with a vengeance.

The three previous wartime changes had seen the basic rate of duty go up by 24, 17 and 16s per barrel. In April 1942 Sir Kingsley Wood piled on the agony. The basic rate leapt up by more than 37s to 118s 1½d, adding not a penny but at least twopence to the price of a pint. A jar of mild at 10d a pint cost double its pre-war price. Cider escaped untouched.

A stunned *Brewers' Journal* could only comment that month: 'The tremendous heights to which taxation of alcoholic beverages has now risen places those creature comforts beyond the reach of sections of our people.' Breweries and pubs had become 'tax-gathering centres collecting gigantic sums.' The Chancellor expected the rise to bring

in a further £48 million in a full year, making the total revenue from beer froth over the £200 million mark. Or would it?

The Brewers' Journal reported in May 1942: 'The public has taken unkindly to the increased duties on beer.' Many were said to be drinking less. Donald McCullough in a session of the Brains' Trust called the new taxation 'the scorched public house policy.' Yet once drinkers had got over the initial shock, they reached for their glasses and carried on as before. At the end of the year the new duty provided a handsome surplus of £14 million over the estimate of £204 million. Demand remained strong even if the beer did not.

It seemed nothing the Chancellor could do during the war could kill the goose which laid the golden eggs. In April 1943 he pushed the basic rate to 138s 4½d, adding a further penny on a pint, and adjusted it marginally higher again in 1944. *The Brewers' Journal* was no longer surprised 'in view of the astounding buoyancy of the revenue from beer.' Sir Kingsley Wood in 1943 expected over £250 million to pour out of the beer pumps. This target was easily exceeded.

By the end of the war the average price of a pint of mild (still the nation's favourite beer) was around a shilling. The duty on beer during the war had increased almost six-fold from a basic rate of 24s to 140s 7½d. It now accounted for a substantial part of the price of a pint.

The beer drinker could hold up his glass and claim with pride that he had done his bit to help win the war by filling the Treasury's chests.

THE BLITZ
Beating the Bombs

The most obvious threat to the brewing industry during the war came from the skies, from the enemy bombers. The rain of terror was expected – but the most feared weapon never arrived.

Despite a political policy of appeasing Hitler, Britain had been rearming since 1935 to counter the growing military might of Germany. Increasingly more and more resources were poured into building aircraft to match the aerial strength of the Luftwaffe. The Spanish Civil War had demonstrated the punitive power of the German planes. Bombers were the new weapons of mass destruction, as had been starkly shown at Guernica, a Spanish village attacked by German bombers on a crowded market day.

But it was only with the Czechoslovakia crisis of 1938 that the British public woke up to the imminent danger of war. Memories came flooding back of the first Great War, and the miles of muddy, bloodied trenches. Old soldiers recalled the misty menace of gas drifting over the lines. Now it was feared the Germans would drop deadly gas bombs on Britain, wiping out local populations. People began to panic.

GAS DRILL: A gas decontamination team practise cleaning up the yard at George's Brewery in Bristol (*Courage Archive*).

MASKED MEN:
A first-aid team at
Watney's Stag Brewery
in London learn how to
tend the wounded
during a gas attack
(*Courage Archive*).

The Pennant, the glossy house magazine of Benskin's Brewery of
Watford, in its April issue in 1938, in the middle of a gentle, jaunty
series of articles about the rebuilding of the **Royal Hotel** at Luton,
the brewing of old ale in Barnstaple and a workers' holiday snapshot
competition, suddenly struck employees with a three-page feature
on poison gas. It made chilling reading.

The real menace is from aircraft. Modern aeroplanes can carry
bombs weighing from a few ounces to a few tons. Some of
these may be comparatively fragile and break up immediately
on striking the ground, thus liberating their poisonous
contents, or they may be of stouter construction, requiring an
explosive charge to open them. A variety of toxic agents may
thus be liberated which act on the human body in various
ways. Gases such as phosgene and chloropicrin affect the
lungs; tear-gases affect the eyes. Organic arsenic compounds
exert their irritant action on the breathing passages, whilst
others of the blistering type, such as mustard gas and lewisite,
will burn the skin and any other part of the body with which
they come in contact.

With comforting reports like this, it was little surprise people were
beginning to panic. At the height of the Czechoslovakia crisis in
September 1938, more than 38 million gas-masks were distributed
to regional centres around Britain. At the time the country had just
44 anti-aircraft guns. No wonder many cheered wildly when
Chamberlain returned from Munich, waving his piece of paper
signed by Hitler and promising peace in our time. But few believed

CRATE ESCAPE: Simond's Brewery at Reading used old beer crates to build their air-raid shelter. Note the number of young boys now working at the brewery (*Courage Archive*).

it would last. Men were called up for military training and the Government introduced a Civil Defence Bill outlining the measures necessary for the defence of the population in the event of war.

Breweries, like other factories, did not wait for the details. They began to busy themselves building air-raid shelters for their workers; some unlikely constructions even being made out of old beer crates. Wardens' sand-bagged posts – some using hop sacks filled with dirt – were set up on the roofs. Fire-fighting and first-aid teams were trained. Anti-gas groups formed. Warning hooters were installed in noisy areas like the clattering bottling halls, where it would be difficult to hear the public sirens.

There was another valuable commodity every brewery had to consider during a raid. Never mind the workers, what about the beer? The *Journal of the Incorporated Brewers Guild*, in an article headlined 'Aerial Attack', warned:

> Every brewer should ask himself what would happen if an employee ran to cover before taking certain necessary steps to avoid disaster whilst mashing, setting taps, sparging, copper boiling, wort running to collecting vessels etc.
>
> No time should be lost in working out a scheme whereby nothing can happen whilst everyone is under cover. In some breweries fire posts have been built for fire parties; similar but smaller posts should be built for the key employee who, because of his action in shutting valves and turning off switches, may not have sufficient time to get to the main shelter.

Deeds and company books were just as crucial, many being locked away in safe deposits. John Smith's of Tadcaster in Yorkshire strangely moved their vital papers to London for safe keeping. Important stocks of malt and hops were dispersed around outlying properties.

Some companies planned well ahead. The technical director of Guinness's new Park Royal Brewery in London, Dr John Webb, was sent on a three-week air-raid precautions course early in 1939 to learn about high explosives, gas warfare and fire fighting. At the same time the company built several underground shelters, each capable of housing 50 people with a telephone connection to the brewery exchange. The basement of the central offices was strengthened with steel girders and plates and a control room installed. Look-out posts were established on the roofs and a dormitory provided for the 12 volunteers on duty every night. Dr Webb even had a direct line at his bedside to the Observer Corps, who would ring him up as soon as enemy aircraft crossed the coast. When war came Guinness was well prepared.

Later, when the bombs started to fall, Guinness moved their accounts department to Twyford Abbey, the prized accounting machines being protected by bales of hops. 'The smell was atrocious', recalled one worker, 'and they had a curious soporific effect'.

Conscription?

" *Didn't you hear* ' *About Turn* '?"
" *No—what about him* ? "

OUT OF STEP: Not everyone took the pre-war games seriously.

The local defence volunteers had arms as Ernest Guinness gave them the weapons he carried on his yacht (now safely moored in Seattle) – a tommy gun, a big-game rifle and a shot-gun. After the war, when the Home Guard was disbanded, the police confiscated these weapons.

One macabre move was blocked. A local authority official called at Park Royal to suggest establishing a large-scale mortuary at the brewery to accommodate the many bodies expected from the London air-raids. This was firmly turned down on the grounds that the brewery was a food factory. However, a fully-equipped 100-bed emergency hospital was established in the basement of Ansells' Brewery in Birmingham, and proved its worth during air-raids in the Midlands, handling hundreds of casualties.

Manchester Corporation suggested to Chester's Brewery early in 1939 that a massive air-raid shelter should be constructed in the Ardwick brewery's cellars, large enough to accommodate 3,000 people. This grandiose scheme was eventually shelved in favour of a more modest and manageable plan. Chester's was not surprised by unusual war-time requests. In the First World War part of the brewery was used for making shell cases.

Other breweries left their preparations late; Watney's Isleworth Brewery only built air-raid tunnels in the allotments alongside the West London plant on the outbreak of war, when concrete rings weighing 2½ tons each were sunk into three 50ft trenches. Each provided seating, lighting, lavatories and running water behind 'gas-proof doors'.

However, Watney's main Stag Brewery in Pimlico, in the heart of the target area of Westminster, geared up early for the death drop from the skies. A trial air-raid was practised in February 1939, using the brewery hooter to send workers scurrying for cover in the cellars. 'Great excitement was caused locally,' recorded the company's *Red Barrel* magazine. In June a new steam whistle was installed to ensure everyone heard the warning. The brewery's fire-fighting and first-aid teams began to practise regularly. Lessons were held in aircraft spotting.

The latter were increasingly important, as in the first jumpy days of war there were many false alarms, disrupting production. Companies like Watney's came to the conclusion that in order to meet demand, they must carry on working during 'alert' periods, and only send their workers to the shelters when their Jerry spotters on the roof positively identified enemy aircraft approaching. Correct identification was vital. The men with the binoculars had to be able to tell a Spitfire from a Stuka at a distance. At night they had to distinguish the engine sound of German raiders. Their colleagues' lives depended on their decision. Some of London's earliest roof spotters were Girl Guides whose keen eyes and ears proved invaluable.

With the introduction of the black-out, windows were painted, screened or boarded up, but this still left the problem of open loading bays, where light would pour out at night or in the early morning

FIRE POWER: A pre-war fire drill (above) at Watney's Stag Brewery looks amateurish compared to the later four-hose team (*Courage Archive*).

gloom. Watney's came up with a bright solution, known as the Palace Street Air Ship. This involved a curtained hood which was lowered onto lorries, allowing them to be loaded after dark without a flicker being revealed outside.

The company had another problem. It still delivered much of its beer by traditional drays. As one of the largest owners of horses in London, Watney's helped the RSPCA organise air-raid precaution procedures for working animals. A leading drayman advised: 'If an air-raid came along, I should make for the nearest side turning, scotch up my wheels, put the bag on the horse and stand by it.' He had no time for drivers who put their own safety first when the bombs fell. 'It is a poor man who can't stand by and hold his horse.'

In the Stag Brewery stables, Watney's put their faith – in goats. There was a belief that these belligerent creatures acted as a calming influence on horses, and that the gentle giants would follow them in time of crisis. The belief was misplaced. Mr C W Benner of the company's solicitors' department recorded that when the bombs dropped: 'The goats, which were thought to pacify alarmed horses, were found scared stiff in a corner, whilst the horses seemed as placid as if nothing was amiss.'

Watney's came to regret locking horns with these voracious animals. One proved almost as destructive as the bombs:

Billy the goat caused some anxiety at times because it was never known what he'd do next; he disappeared for some days, until he was found by a gateman in the wastepaper store having a good feed of old cheques and accounts. Then again he wandered to the engineers' department and removed and ate the time cards. . . .

And everywhere in this new unreal world, strange squads of men in rubber suits and gas-masks began to practise scrubbing down the brewery yard as part of their decontamination drill after a gas attack. Everyone had to carry their own personal box, containing their own gas-mask. 'Don't be caught without it,' warned the authorities. 'Your first time could be your last.' Budgies and canaries became popular pets as it was believed they would provide an early warning of gas in the air.

Guinness at Park Royal initiated gas-mask working periods, when brewery and office staff were required to wear their masks for 15 minutes while carrying on their duties – much to the alarm of unsuspecting visitors from their Dublin brewery. In towns and cities gas detectors were set up in the streets.

IN CASE OF AIR RAID

The ground floor of the Bottling Store is recommended as the safest place.

Take your Gas Masks and bring torches if possible.

BOXING CLEVER: Breweries reminded their staff to always carry their gas-mask boxes (left), but not everyone used them for the correct purpose. Some kept cards there (*Courage Archive*).

Warning!   *Take cover!*   *All clear!*
So that's what the little box is for!

The Ministry of Food issued a booklet entitled 'Food and its Protection Against Poison Gas.' Gas identification officers, usually qualified chemists, were appointed in every district. Their job in the event of a raid was to visit affected sites, quickly identify the gas and advise what action must be taken.

If beer has been contaminated, for example, in an open fermenting vessel by droplets of mustard gas or any similar blister gas, it would have to be condemned. Again for beer stored in casks, where the outsides have been heavily contaminated by mustard gas, there is a risk of the gas being absorbed by the wood and ultimately reaching the contents.

Yet the seeping terror never came – but all the other precautions proved vital. The gas bombs did not fall but in their place came thousands of high-explosives and fierce incendiaries which caused widespread destruction. Flying bombs and rockets followed later in the war.

BAGGING UP: The gatehouse at Watney's Stag Brewery in Pimlico disappears beneath sand bags at the outbreak of war (*Courage Archive*).

One extreme temperance campaigner, the Rev. J Norton at the Chester and Warrington Methodist Synod, said all the brewery fire and sand-bag precautions were unnecessary. He claimed that German airmen would not bomb breweries and maltings in Britain 'because Hitler knows that if Britons go on drinking at the present rate we shall lose the war.' Some Luftwaffe pilots obviously ignored the Fuehrer's instructions, though it was claimed that the Hull Brewery survived the bombing because its tall chimney provided a useful landmark for German planes approaching the east coast.

Devenish's Weymouth brewery was put out of action for two years following a blitz on the Dorset seaside town, close to the Portland naval base, on 11 August, 1940. 'The brewery has been severely damaged in a vital part, the structure of the brewhouse; the copper room, hop-back and under-back all suffering heavily, whilst the main portion of the front office is completely demolished.' The Devenish directors were informed: 'It will not be possible to rebuild or to brew for some considerable time.'

Many south coast ports, particularly those with naval bases like Plymouth and Portsmouth, were badly hit. In Southampton Cooper's East Street Brewery was severely damaged, but brewer Stephen Clarke devised a special 'pressure fermentation' system to enable brewing to continue. Later in the war crippled Cooper's was taken over by Watney's. Bristol and South Wales were also heavily attacked.

The more distant North-West did not avoid punishment. Liverpool was plastered. Bent's Brewery was put out of action and many bottling stores in the docks destroyed, including those of Guinness and Wrexham Lager. Mr Price, the head brewer of the Birkenhead Brewery, was killed in the blitz.

Manchester did not escape the dark shadow of the bombers, either. On 22 December, 1940, the peace of the last Sunday before Christmas was shattered by a heavy air raid. A large bomb exploded in Wilburn Street outside Groves & Whitnall's Salford brewery, damaging the cooperage, cask-washing plant and garage. The blast also blew off the roof of the main buildings.

The assault on the city was relentless. The next night a landmine, dropped by parachute, hit the brewery offices. 'Nothing was left of that fine range of buildings . . . except a great crater and a pile of debris strewn across Regent Road,' recalled the chairman, Keith Groves. Two people were killed in the blast, the caretaker and a member of the works' fire brigade. A blaze raged after the main explosion and the debris smouldered for more than a week. Regent Road was impassable for three days.

The destruction of the offices meant that the company lost all its trading books and records. Many of these were eventually recovered from the debris over a period of several weeks. Some, however, were totally destroyed and others badly damaged. It took many months of painstaking work to decipher the remains and build up missing details. Keith Groves explained:

WRECKED: Groves and Whitnall's Brewery in Salford after it was bombed out of action in December 1940.

Fortunately the concrete and steel wing of the Globe Works, new in 1939, withstood the shock, thus saving much of the bottling plant and machinery. Incendiary bombs, however, struck this building and the adjoining wine and spirit stores, starting many fires, all of which were put out by the Globe Works Fire Brigade, who stuck to their task until well into the following day and prevented still greater loss.

Luckily, all the brewing plant remained intact and Groves & Whitnall were brewing their 'Red Rose' ales and stout again by 17 January, 1941. Local residents were particularly glad that they lived near the brewery – several hundred sheltered in the cellars during the bombing.

Another Manchester brewery was less fortunate. Boddingtons' Strangeways Brewery was severely damaged by incendiary bombs in the same Christmas blitz in 1940, and put out of action for a long period. The steel city of Sheffield suffered even worse, with a double blow. Rawson's Pond Street Brewery and Tomlinson's Anchor Brewery were both flattened in air raids in 1940. In Sunderland, Robsons was bombed out of brewing the following year.

Sometimes the brewers themselves were to blame for the explosions. Many had neglected their plant during the depressed years of the 1930s and the strain of the war proved too much for some ancient equipment. In 1937 Bill Kitchen, head brewer of the Tower Brewery at Tadcaster in Yorkshire, had warned his directors that all three boiling coppers were obsolete and dangerous. In May 1944, his worst fears were realised. The No.3 copper blew up without any assistance from enemy aircraft.

Yet, despite the widespread destruction, morale-raising beer supplies were maintained, as breweries rolled out the barrels to support their stricken fellows. In Weymouth, near neighbours John Groves & Sons and Dorset brewers Eldridge Pope supplied Devenish's pubs while its brewery was out of action. Eldridge Pope was repaying an old debt. Devenish had helped them out almost two decades before when their Dorchester brewery was destroyed by fire in 1922. Later the Devenish directors presented the John Groves board with a silver salver 'in appreciation of services kindly rendered during 1940-1942.'

Elsewhere emergency arrangements were put into action. Across the country, brewers agreed to aid each other in a crisis, supplying each other's pubs if their plant was put out of action. Old rivalries were put aside and everyone worked for the common good to overcome tremendous difficulties. Often it was not just the question of brewing enough beer which proved a problem, but other issues like transport or cask washing which were the weakest links in the chain.

Mr F A Simonds, chairman of Simonds of Reading, praised the new mood of help-your-neighbour at the company's annual shareholders' meeting at the end of 1941. He recounted that in the spring his southern brewing group was badly affected when their Devonport brewery in Plymouth was partially destroyed in an air-raid.

We were unable to meet the full requirements of our customers, but fortunately a number of brewery firms – no fewer than 14 in all – came to our aid and are still helping us. They quite voluntarily supplied us with a weekly barrelage or placed their brewery at our disposal for one or two brews a week, and thus did much to relieve our embarrassment.

Sometimes the arrangements became permanent. In Sheffield Henry Tomlinson's wrecked Anchor Brewery in Bramall Lane was supplied with beer by local neighbours Carter, Milner & Bird of the Hope Brewery. In 1942 they merged to form Hope & Anchor Breweries Ltd. This war-time creation became a potent force after the conflict when it marketed its popular Jubilee Stout across the country.

In Manchester the story was the same, with a total of 22 local rivals rallying round to supply Boddingtons' houses for many months. Groves & Whitnall also benefited from this new spirit of co-operation, as Keith Groves recalled:

A few days after the 'Blitz' a meeting was held of all Manchester, Salford and neighbouring brewers, who arranged that help should be given to firms which had suffered. Nine other breweries supplied us until we were again in full production. In later bombings other local breweries were damaged and we, in our turn, supplied them with part of their requirements.

The morale of all the staff and employees, throughout this difficult period, was beyond praise. During the following days many of them, in intervals of searching the still smouldering ruins, took turns in relieving the fire service on the hoses.

For several months in bitter weather, the men and girls of the bottling works carried on their task of producing the firm's bottled goods under the most severe conditions. About one-third of them worked totally in the open air, with their only comfort the doubtful warmth of coke braziers; the remainder in roofless and windowless buildings.

When Bent's Brewery in Liverpool was severely damaged in an air raid in 1941, the company was fortunate in having taken over Gartside's Brewery of Ashton-under-Lyne just before the war broke out. All brewing was transferred there. Morgan's Brewery in Norwich was also destroyed by enemy action in June 1942, but the company was able to continue brewing as it owned Eyre's Brewery at King's Lynn.

The distinctive flavour of Morgan's East Anglian ales was not lost, as the day before the bombers burnt down the company's Old Brewery in King Street, Norwich, a small Suffolk brewery had called to pick up a supply of yeast. The brewery was Adnams of Southwold – which continues to use Morgan's yeast in their famous beers to this day.

Some previously unwanted plants were rushed back into production. When the Cornbrook Brewery in Manchester received a direct hit and was put out of action for two years late in 1940 – much to the annoyance of the company which had just completed a new bottling hall a year before – the firm early in 1941 leased the Royal Oak Brewery in Stockport from Walker & Homfrays of Salford. Later in 1943 this same site was let to London brewers Whitbread.

This tale of fighting against the odds was nowhere repeated to more dramatic effect than in London. The capital city was menaced by wave after wave of bombers, being hit for 76 nights in a row from 7 September, 1940, and then bombed more sporadically for a further six months.

On 1 October, 1940, a 1,000lb bomb hit Barclay's historic brewery in Southwark, exploding right in the heart of the brewhouse and wrecking three out of the five coppers and mash tuns. Altogether eight high-explosive bombs and on 32 occasions incendiaries fell on the buildings, the brewery fire brigade having to put out 18 fires.

The neighbouring Courage brewery, next to Tower Bridge, had its roof blown off and river wall shattered. 'But the Victorian builders had done their job well and the old structure held the waters of the Thames,' declared the company's historian, John Pudney, in *A Draught of Contentment*. Only two days production were lost and the company expanded its brewing capacity later in the war by buying Hodgson's Kingston Brewery in 1943.

Over the river at Whitbread's Chiswell Street premises, the hectic,

BLITZED: Bomb damage at Mann's Whitechapel Brewery in London (*Courage Archive*).

SURVIVOR: Whitbread's Chiswell Street Brewery stands intact among a sea of rubble (*Whitbread Archive*).

heroic efforts of the London brewer's own workers somehow kept this ancient brewery intact when almost all other buildings around were reduced to rubble in one of the most intensive bombing campaigns of the war.

On the night of Sunday, 29 December, 1940 – a week after the Manchester blitz – hundreds of thousands of incendiary bombs rained on the heart of London. The ancient Guildhall and eight Wren churches went up in flames. Acres of offices, shops and homes were flattened. Paternoster Row, with its bookshops and historic Chapter House, was levelled. At one time a single square mile in the old City contained 4,000 fires. Among all this destruction, Whitbread's Brewery battled to survive. The logbook of the company's fire brigade recalls the full horror:

> The air-raid warning sounded at 6.10pm. The north and south observation posts were manned by auxiliary firemen as fire-watchers; and within a few minutes of their arrival they reported incendiary bombs in the cask-washing yard and on

the cafeteria roof. The fire pump was immediately started up and men detailed to deal with the bombs.

Before the first few incendiary bombs in the north yard could be put out, another basketful dropped on the north side, falling on the unloading banks, the cask and coal stores, cask-washing shed roof, cooperage, hop loft and open yard. These bombs were dealt with by sand, stirrup pumps and fire hoses. All the bombs and the fires resulting from this basket were quickly put out.

In the first half-hour of the raid other bombs fell on the south side, the engineers' roof, Whitecross Street and many buildings near the brewery. Later more incendiaries and high-explosive bombs were dropped by the raiders. Only incendiary bombs fell on the brewery premises. Some of these fell on the hop loft, the painters' shop, the finings house, the brewers' house, the south-side hop store, and again on many buildings near the brewery. A number of these bombs did not ignite and were picked up and placed in sand.

By this time scores of fires were raging in the City on premises which had no fire watchers; whole streets were ablaze. Due to the number of fires and severance of water mains by high-explosive bombs and falling buildings, there was an acute shortage of liquor (water), and the fire pump had to depend on the reserve supply of liquor in the brewery tanks.

The danger to the brewery from other fires in the vicinity was far greater than that from the incendiary bombs which fell on the buildings, and liquor had to be conserved to prevent fires spreading from across the adjoining streets to the brewery. The fire which eventually gutted the hop store could, without doubt, have been kept under control, had enough liquor been available. The fire on the Counting House roof was put out with extinguishers. Great efforts were made to prevent the fire spreading from the west-side of Whitecross Street, the east-side of Milton Street and the south-side of Silk Street. Whitbread's fire brigade was working from the roof of the brewery buildings.

During all this time the raid was still in progress. Our fighters were heard overhead, and the noise of machine-gun and cannon-shell duels could be heard. The barrage-balloons were as clearly visible from the light of the numerous fires as in the day-time, and during this period no assistance was received from the London Fire Brigade or the Auxiliary Fire Service. In fact, assistance was given from the brewery fire brigade to them, and two of the brewery fire brigade sent to help outside were highly commended by the police.

The stables in Garrett Street also received a number of incendiary bombs, which were dealt with by the stable fire-brigade. And as a number of buildings near the stables were burning dangerously, the horses were moved to the brewery by the stable staff and some volunteers from the brewery, each man taking two horses. They were first tied up against the middle stage but as the hop loft above caught alight soon after, they were then led over to the south stage under cover of the malt hoist. Blinkers were put on all the horses because of their fear of fire. Similarly vehicles in the north yard had to be transferred to points of less danger several times. During the night not a single horse was injured or lorry damaged. The 'All Clear' was sounded at 11.30, and at this time the fires in the City had not reached their height.

In the cold light of the following morning, the damage was assessed. The biggest loss was the hop loft, which had been destroyed with the loss of 1,800 pockets of hops, worth over £40,000. The co-operage and timber store was also gutted, as was the engineers' building. But the vital brewhouse was safe, only the roof over the No.6 fermenting room was burnt out – resulting in the loss of 1,000 barrels of mild ale. In addition, one cooler and the little-mourned excise office were destroyed.

Miraculously, there were no serious casualties, though 130 men were attended to for minor wounds by the brewery's own first-aid squad. Some dray horses had strayed during the nightmare night, but in the dawn they returned, wandering nervously back to their stables, half dazed, along with other horses from surrounding businesses. The new friends settled in together in the stalls.

The survival of the horses was seen as vital since, following the acquisition of many lorries by the armed forces and severe petrol rationing, they provided essential transport. Mann's Brewery in the East End had not been so fortunate. Their stables were hit by a land mine, killing or maiming many fine shires.

Though the gas supply was cut, there was some electric power and Whitbread's brewing plant was operational – if sufficient water could be obtained. Outside the brewery, the picture was totally different. The whole area around the walls was a ruined wasteland.

DESTRUCTION: The view across the City of London from Whitbread's Brewery after the raid of December 29, 1940 (*Whitbread Archive*).

The roads were unusable for 24 hours owing to the massive craters and scattered debris – and the fire-fighting operations still in progress.

Brewing started again within four days on Thursday, 2 January. There was, however, one burning problem which took longer to extinguish. The malt tower had been set alight during the raid, and 1,200 quarters of malt in one loft smoked for days. 'The malt smouldering in No.3 loft was removed with great difficulty. Men worked day and night until the danger to the building and to the malt in the other lofts was removed. It was not until the following Sunday that the danger was passed.'

The blackened, burnt malt was dumped in a huge mountain in the brewery yard. Rain ruined it further; it was of no use for brewing. But nothing was wasted during the war – so it was sent to a firm of biscuit makers.

The brewery's survival in a sea of destruction was so remarkable, some refused to believe it, as Whitbread director Sydney Nevile discovered on the night of the great raid:

When I got near Chiswell Street, I was stopped by the police and told that the whole district had been devastated and that there was nothing left. However, they let me through so that I could judge the extent of the disaster. Before I reached it, I saw the brewery standing practically undamaged, amid a desert of still blazing ruins. Harry Whitbread's foresight in establishing a house fire brigade had indeed paid big dividends.

The brigade had been helped by an army of volunteers who sprang out of the brewery's cellars, as Nevile revealed in his memoirs *Seventy Rolling Years:*

When bombing began and passenger transport to the brewery was difficult, we housed many of our workers in the cellars and indeed opened these cellars to many in the neighbour-hood who sought refuge.

The provision of sleeping accommodation at short notice taxed our ingenuity, and provision of proper beds was out of the question. However, we had plenty of scaffold poles, so we called our scaffolders together and with the aid of hop pockets (the sacks in which hops are baled) which happened to be of exactly the width needed, we erected several hundred berths in two tiers in the cellars in less than 48 hours, and this met the occasion. Roughly 200 of our men slept in this part of the cellars, while in other corners many of our staff and usually two directors also remained in case of emergency.

With their help, the brewery had beaten the bombs.

Watney's Stag Brewery next to Victoria Station also survived, though the roof watchers suffered many anxious moments. 'It's like sitting on the bull's eye of a darts board whilst play is in progress,' recalled one. Walter Serocold in *The Story of Watneys*, published just after the war, recorded:

Many aerial combats were witnessed when looking eastwards to the Thames mouth; often did the Spitfire or Hurricane pilot prove his superiority over his enemy equivalent and over the heavy bombers which seemed to come in masses and hordes. So much so, that the enemy tactics were changed, his losses were too great; and then began the sneak raids in the dark. The incidents came thick and fast.

Excitement prevailed when a lone enemy aircraft was pursued over London and disintegrated in the air above the brewery, its remains falling on the roof and in the yard, whilst the engine crashed by Victoria Station.

Many dark nights were lit up by tracer bullets and the dull thud of unexploded bombs.

A delayed action bomb fell behind the stable wall but could not be found till dawn, when it was seen nose upwards like a shark's head. The bomb disposal unit was called, it was examined, and it was forecast that it would explode 23 hours later. It did, and took the building in Victoria Street with it.

Another heavy missile plunged through the box store and penetrated the tunnel of the district railway line beneath the brewery.

Buckingham Palace was hit and news reports from Germany seemed to suggest that this was an accident caused by some oil storage tanks in the vicinity. Could it be the company's oil tanks? Just in case, the painters were put to the job of camouflage painting and, when finished, they looked very pretty indeed. But it was sarcastically said that they would then be much easier to see from the air!

Later in the war came the flying bomb.

They could be picked out on a clear day some 10 miles distant, when they were watched carefully, with one finger readily poised on the alarm button. In dull weather one had to rely on good directional hearing; the motor had a coarse note and it cut out before the bomb dived to do its dirty work. This did not undermine morale as the enemy had hoped, and often one heard the London boys chanting: 'Praise the Lord, but keep the engine running!'

One 'doodle bug', as the flying bombs were known, missed the chimney stack at Watney's Mortlake Brewery by inches. Finally came Hitler's last desperate throw for victory – the V2 rocket – about which there was little anyone could do except pray. 'It travelled faster than sound, so it exploded first and you heard it coming afterwards!'

On the road life was no less dangerous for the draymen. Three men 'were travelling in a westerly direction when a bomb dropped in front of their lorry, lifting it some feet into the air. It finally came to earth in the crater made by the bomb,' reported Watney's *Red Barrel* magazine in November 1940. 'Although badly shaken the three men were able to smash their way out of the cab . . . The lorry was eventually pulled out of the crater and went, under its own steam, on its way to Mortlake, which says a lot for the Leyland lorry.'

Some draymen became heroes.

F Monk and driver E Bryant also have a tale of the road to

ON PATROL: Watney's Home Guard unit provided valuable back-up for the armed forces.

tell. They were delivering tank beer to one of the company's **Rising Suns** in the East End when they heard the familiar screech of a falling bomb. In the nick of time they dived under the lorry and were unhurt. The bomb fell quite close by and demolished a house. On crawling out Monk and Bryant were able to assist in rescuing people from the debris, they being personally responsible for the rescue of two women, a baby and an elderly man.

The constant threat from above not only shredded people's nerves, the dray horses were also traumatised. Some were killed. On 11 May, 1941, a bomb hit the brewery stables killing 12 horses. The survivors were moved to the Royal Mews. Thus it was no surprise when the *Red Barrel* reported in July 1941:

Buckingham Palace Road was roped off for nearly an hour on the evening of Tuesday, the 10th of June, when two of the company's horses attached to a dray, for no apparent reason, bolted from the Stag Yard where they were being unharnessed by driver Carter. The dray crashed into the shop front of Maison Georges, the hairdressers. One of the horses, which became wedged in a door, was so badly injured in its struggles that it had to be destroyed. The other animal went up the stairs to the first landing.

Eventually it was calmed and brought down, backwards.

STANDING DOWN: Watney's Home Guard takes the final salute from brewery chairman Colonel Serocold.

Watney's did not only deliver the beer through the ruined streets, watch the skies and wait for the bombs to drop. Under the chairman Colonel O P Serocold, a Home Guard squad was formed at the Stag Brewery. He was continuing a long company tradition. One of the London breweries which made up the group, Reid's, had organised a volunteer unit to defend the country against Napoleon in 1801.

Unlike many of the Dad's Army brigades, Watney's was not short of transport, having use of the company's drays for training. The platoon consisted of 60 men and 36 heavy vehicles, plus motorcycles, and became part of London's reserve transport unit in an emergency. Serious training was carried out with exercises against regular army units, with mock battles in Epping Forest and on Wimbledon Common.

'Many were the miles traversed as a result of a misread map reference, and much ammunition was spent in becoming proficient in the use of Sten guns, anti-tank weapons and rifles,' recorded Walter Serocold in *The Story of Watneys*. A rifle range was even opened at the brewery in April 1940. The feared invasion never came and in December 1944 the platoon was disbanded.

Guinness also formed a Home Guard unit at Park Royal and on one famous occasion the men hunted a reported parachutist round and round the reservoirs until, when cornered near the malt store, the enemy turned out to be a very frightened sheep.

Some 20 high-explosive bombs and showers of incendiaries fell on Park Royal, most of which bounced off the solid concrete roofs of the modern buildings which looked from the air like a major power

HISTORY DESTROYED: All that was left of the historic Brewers' Hall

station. One raid, recalled under-brewer Des O'Brien, was frustrated by one employee 'running along the vathouse roof and drop-kicking the incendiaries over the parapet.'

Only one bomb caused serious fatalities when it plunged through the roof of the ice house, killing four men on duty. The case of another bomb, which lodged in the corner of a packed air-raid shelter without exploding, was placed in the office entrance as a gruesome souvenir. Park Royal was also struck by a doodlebug (flying bomb), as Des O'Brien vividly remembered:

> Big Bill Donovan, my shift foreman, had started the mash with me when the air-raid siren went off. All the men immediately decamped to the shelter but, knowing the potential difficulties of a halted, clogged mash, Bill and I decided to carry on, running from one mill to another to control the flow. Suddenly there was an almighty explosion and everything loose in the brewhouse came tumbling down including all the black-out panels. There were clouds of mill dust everywhere. A doodle bug had hit next door. Bill, all six-foot-six of him, said very quickly, 'I think we'd better go, sir' – and we ran.

These experiences were typical of many London brewers. Young's Brewery in Wandsworth was hit several times as were Charrington and Mann's in the East End. Worst affected of all was Taylor Walker's Barley Mow Brewery in Limehouse. This was so severely damaged in March 1941, that it was put out of action for 18 months, not resuming production until August 1942. In the meantime beer was supplied by its subsidiary Cannon Brewery in Clerkenwell.

The Cannon's offices in St John Street also became the home of the Brewers' Company after the historic Brewers' Hall in the City was totally destroyed on 29 December, 1940. (Taylor Walker's chairman Commander Redmond McGrath was master of the company throughout the war.) The Brewers' Company could toast a history going back over 500 years. It was no stranger to destruction. The original hall had been destroyed in the Great Fire of London and rebuilt in 1673. Now nothing survived of the old Stuart hall except a few pieces of leaded glass from the window panes. Fortunately its ancient records were saved, being housed elsewhere. Other papers survived in a safe, though the edges of the pages were charred by the intense heat.

Further east the rain of terror on Ind Coope's Romford Brewery in Essex was recorded in their house magazine *The Red Hand* in January 1947. It recorded how air-attack warnings were sounded almost daily from the start of September 1940, for eight months:

13.10.40: Two oil bombs, one in yard other on rail tracks to ale stores; this one did not explode, yard one blows out all windows in engineers' office and boiler house. Patrol man puts out.

16.10.40: Heavy attack on Romford town. Bomb in London Road (front of brewery) showers area with tarmac.

23.10.40: High explosive drops on recreation room, also demolishes part of laboratory and some of B Grant & Co's wine & spirit stores.

8.12.40: A parachute bomb drops behind boiler house at about 11pm (Sunday). Every door, window and most roofs of brewery and fermenting room and B Grant's stores are completely wrecked. A large brew was in progress but as they could not have a light (due to blackout) copper fires are drawn and everything left to daylight. Temperature did not drop too much and brew was OK. Mr Neville Thompson (chairman) turned up next day. A quarter-ton anvil was blown over the three-storey White Hart (the brewery tap), over shops and into an air-raid shelter.

3.3.41: Raids continue and an AA (Ack-Ack) shell falls in B Grant's premises and demolishes a modern convenience – no-one in at time!

19/20.4.41: Town has worst attack. Forty-four people killed and 2,000 houses destroyed. Brewery not hit.

21.1.44: Early morning raid of incendiary bombs. Bottling stores burn furiously. Brewery own fire-brigade keep under

HOW DARE THEY: George's managing director Arthur Hadley surveys the hole in the Bristol brewery's roof left by a 100lb unexploded bomb in November 1940 (*Courage Archive*).

control until NFS (National Fire Service) arrive. Put fire out by 8am. Store mainly destroyed. A bomb which was lodged in the rush roof of the hop loft bursts into flames, spreads rapidly to whole of hop store. Contents (700 pockets of hops) destroyed. Mr Neville Thompson arrives again and within two weeks bottling again in part rebuilt bottling store; later on a new hop store built.

18.4.44: Midnight raid. Hundreds of incendiaries are dropped on the brewery. A terrifying night. Every part of brewery seems to be in flames. Fires tackled by brewery fire-brigade and got under control except roof of fermenting room, which is eventually done with assistance of NFS. Large hole in roof covered in tarpaulins for six months and continue to use fermenting vessels. Fortunately yeast keeps OK. In this fire bottling hall is completely destroyed, also roof of conditioning and chilling rooms. Six months later a new bottling hall built.

These stark details illustrate how breweries had to battle to beat the bombs and keep on brewing. At the other end of the beer line, many pubs were just as badly blasted.

PUBS IN THE FRONT LINE
Serving Up Good Cheer

If the breweries were the prime suppliers of liquid morale during the war, the front-line troops in keeping everyone's chins up were the men and women running the pubs of Britain.

When Winston Churchill uttered his wartime words, 'This was their finest hour', he was not thinking about licensees and their staff. But the famous quote applies just as much to those manning the bars as to those manning the barricades against Hitler's army. When the bombs fell, many battled on against tremendous odds.

Dover, which stared the enemy across the Channel full in the face, was within easy reach of German guns as well as their aircraft. Whitbread in their house magazine made special mention of 'two dauntless ladies', Mrs Le Gros of the **Duchess of Kent** and Mrs Wigg of **York House** in the bombarded port:

Nothing Hitler could do would move them from their determination to carry on. If the ground floor was destroyed, one apparently just moved upstairs while repairs were carried out. If the top of the house was knocked off, it just seemed

FATAL HIT:
The landlord Mr Goodman King was killed when this Taylor Walker house, the **Lord Stanley** in Hackney, was destroyed.

obvious to move down again. In that spirit they carried on while houses next door fell one after another.

Watney's board had nothing but praise for its licensees during the 'death and destruction which have been rained nightly on London.' The *Red Barrel* recorded their appreciation in October 1940:

The directors have heard with admiration of the fine spirit displayed by tenants, staff and employees who have sustained injury and loss. Many licensees have pressed for the early erection of some form of shanty or for some adaptation of what is left of their premises so that they may carry on the good work of providing for the needs of their neighbourhood, whilst others have risen nobly to the occasion in providing shelter and food for those suddenly deprived of their homes.

The air-raid wardens for Southwark had written to the brewery praising 'the great service' rendered by licensee Andy Chismon of **The Giraffe** in Amelia Street after the area had been devastated:

Many people were rendered homeless and wounded, and this great little man threw open his premises, making his saloon bar a casualty clearing station and the other part of the premises a refuge for the people during this awful night. He and his good wife then supplied these unfortunate people with over 400 cups of tea, with cigarettes etc and allowed them to remain on his premises until the morning, then supplying over 60 breakfasts without accepting one halfpenny during the whole of this time.

Another licensee, Mr W Lindley, who ran the **Star and Garter** in Rotherhithe – which was completely destroyed in an air-raid, killing his wife and severely injuring him – wrote from hospital to Watney's board asking them to put up any old shack on the ruined site so that when he came out of hospital, he could carry on as before.

The December issue of the *Red Barrel* magazine reported the stories of two unnamed houses. One manager of an ancient thirteenth century pub, Mr R E Thorpe, wrote down his experiences during one week, starting at 7.45pm one evening:

Police informed me that there was an incendiary bomb blazing on my roof. It had apparently penetrated between the party wall to a depth of four feet and the rafters were well alight. Sand was applied until the supply was exhausted, followed by water which had to be carried up two flights of stairs. . . . Eventually our efforts were rewarded. The fire died down and although the wall was still very hot the arrival of the fire-

MISSED:
Watney's Brewery
Tap narrowly
survived this raid
(*Courage Archive*).

brigade soon made everything safe. . . . Meanwhile the house was carrying on down below and customers were quite unconcerned about any danger except to inquire of me 'How's the fire going, landlord?' or 'Is it out yet?' Numerous offers of refreshment were made to me amid plenty of good-natured chaff.

The following morning a high-explosive bomb blew out the windows and damaged the ceilings but 'the staff were eager to start their duties and the scarred house was doing business as usual at opening time, unperturbed by the earlier morning experience.' The following Saturday evening 'another very near bomb gave us a bad shaking,' he wrote. 'We turned out for the night under police orders, but Sunday morning back to the bar as usual, and smiling too.'

Licensees were determined to maintain 'business as usual' as far as possible. A survey by *The Brewers' Journal* in September 1940, found that 90 per cent of pubs examined on a tour of London remained open during an air-raid warning. 'The type of licensed premises we found closed was the larger houses, where control of customers and staff in an emergency would obviously have been more difficult.' In some of the smaller pubs 'we found trading confined to certain bars which occupied the most sheltered position.'

One who had half his house blown away, was reported punctually at opening time to be 'found behind the bar of that part of the premises still standing, serving drinks and cracking jokes as usual – but behind him, instead of the rows of shining bottles, was a gaping void.'

However, in the evening the story tended to be different. The *Journal* reported the following month: 'At the time of writing only a small proportion of licensed houses in the London area open at night or, if they remain open, enjoy extensive trade.' Many customers were not venturing out after dark into the dangerous streets. In Manchester the licensed trade agreed that as a temporary measure all pubs should close by 9.30pm; in Liverpool a curfew of 9pm was imposed.

Some customers were not always so understanding about the problems facing the trade. One sued Chiswick brewers Fuller, Smith & Turner when the ceiling of the **Admiral Nelson** pub at Whitton, Hounslow, fell in, breaking his right arm. Frank Claxton alleged that 'the ceiling was of faulty or hasty construction,' but the judge found that the fall was due to vibration from gunfire, and the case against the brewery and the licensee, Mrs A Cox, was dismissed.

The appearance of some houses was changed not only by the enemy's bombs. As fear of invasion grew in the summer of 1940, signposts were removed to confuse invading troops. The names of prominent pubs were also often taken down, as many old inns provided landmarks, some being marked on maps. 'Though we should imagine that it would not be in the national interest to remove the legend "Burton on Draught" from **The Bell** at Nether Backwash as it might mislead the unwelcome visitor,' commented *The Brewers' Journal*. A few houses were even camouflaged like **The Northover** at Downham, Essex, which was painted in drab mottled shapes.

In these trying times, ingenuity was often needed to dowse the flames of war. When Mr and Mrs Paull of the **Marshal Keate** in Poplar found there was no water to fight the fires caused by incendiary bombs, they put out the blaze with beer drawn from the wood. 'A truly remarkable piece of quick thinking which undoubtedly saved

DEFIANT: St Paul's Cathedral stands unscathed, along with Whitbread's **King Lud** pub in the heart of London.

the house,' commented the *Red Barrel* magazine. Other Watney landlords brightened up their ruined premises to lift their customers' spirits.

Harold Benson's pub was badly damaged by a bomb, the landlord being knocked out by the blast 'and awoke to find himself in Charing Cross Hospital where he had five stitches in his head.' He quickly left the ward to return home.

He expected to find the house in ruins but to his joy and amazement found the four walls standing although there was a fair amount of internal damage. By this time the staff were busy removing the debris and all agreed to go to it. So with goodwill and 'To hell with Hitler' spirit they went to it wholeheartedly. From Tuesday's absolute chaos, perfect order was restored to the house, which was in full working order by Thursday.

In fact, customers noted with pleasure that their local had been much improved. 'Fresh October roses were profuse everywhere, flower baskets were hanging from the roof . . . there were hurricane lamps, warmers and the whole place spelt comfort.

Such uplifting tales of war-time spirit could not hide the massive scale of destruction. Whitbread estimated that 90 per cent of their properties in London suffered war damage. During the blitz 565 of their pubs in the capital were hit, with 78 of them either completely destroyed or so badly wrecked that trading ceased. Later in the rocket and flying bomb attacks, 549 pubs were damaged, 36 of them seriously. Altogether there were 2,254 war damage incidents.

'At one time nearly every day had its quota of casualties and incidents – houses completely destroyed or badly damaged, ceilings down or windows blasted,' reported Whitbread's house magazine after the war. 'First-aid repairs had to be carried out immediately, damage had to be assessed and claims tabulated.'

Watney's had 84 pubs reduced to rubble with a further 25 so severely damaged that they had to be closed indefinitely. The names of the 18 tenants and their wives who lost their lives were commemorated on a plaque in the offices at the Stag Brewery, unveiled by chairman Colonel Serocold in November 1945.

East London brewers Charrington's were even harder hit. The company owned a third of the pubs in the City of London and dominated many other heavily bombed areas. It was estimated that over 12 per cent of their pubs were blasted out of existence. 'Between the period from July 1940 to June 1941 the company's property was involved in 1,590 "incidents", as they were euphemistically described at the time, and suffered the total loss of 48 houses,' recorded the firm's historian L A G Strong in *A Brewer's Progress* in 1957.

'The next acute period of damage fell during the flying bomb attacks of June, July and August 1944. In these three months alone, Charrington's had to cope with 950 incidents,' added the book. Altogether throughout the war their 'Toby Jug' houses suffered 5,743 times, with 149 pubs completely destroyed. And it was not just the enemy the brewery had to contend with, as Mr Strong wrote with feeling:

> By an irony of circumstance experienced in other businesses besides brewing, the company had to defend some of its damaged premises from total destruction at the hands of local authorities, and restore them by the best means in its power.

Anything more than patch and board was not allowed. Major repairs and building work was prohibited. Work on new pubs had been suspended when war broke out. Work on the half-complete **Lightbowne Hotel** in Moston, Manchester, had stopped when

Germany invaded Poland. It took months of wrangling by Chester's Brewery to gain permission to put a roof on to preserve the fabric. The hotel was not finally finished until 1954. Another pub, the **Duke of Wellington** in Chatham, Kent, was more fortunate. Only its large cellar had been completed when war broke out – so this was converted into a safe bar known as **The Underground.**

Once the bombs dropped, brewers were constantly concerned that they would lose the licences of closed or lost houses. Young's of Wandsworth in South-West London, who had 10 of their 135 pubs totally demolished during the war, built temporary huts on the bomb sites to continue to serve their customers – and hang on to the licences.

The German bombers had blasted a wide path for those wanting fewer but better pubs. Or as *The Brewers' Journal* more graphically put it in March 1941: 'The jackals of teetotal opportunism will assuredly be found amongst the ruins of England's stricken licensed houses.'

Some cities were ripe for reform, having seen whole areas reduced to rubble. In Southampton, 92 licensed premises had been bombed out of business by the end of 1940; in neighbouring Portsmouth, 73

SEA OF DESTRUCTION: A quarter of Swansea's pubs were destroyed in the air attacks on the South Wales port (*Western Mail*).

had suffered a similar fate. In Plymouth, almost a quarter of the port's pubs had been closed by enemy action. The chief constable told the city's annual brewster session early in 1942 that out of 431 licensed premises, 104 were closed. In Hull, 78 were shut down, and Swansea lost a quarter of its licensed premises in the blitz.

Many famous pubs disappeared. The most notable was probably **The George** at Portsmouth, the rambling old coaching inn where Lord Nelson spent his last hours ashore in September 1805, before sailing away for his fatal victory at Trafalgar. 'The George was a warrior's inn. It had seen much of wars and preparations for wars – and it was perhaps not unfitting that its end should be through war,' commented Richard Keverne in the third edition of *Tales of Old Inns* published in 1949. All that was left of the old **George** was the wall by the archway through which Nelson walked for the last time – and on it the plaque recording the event.

Coventry lost many of its pubs as well as its cathedral in the blitz. None were more mourned than the historic **King's Head**, though one relic was saved. The night porter dashed back into the blazing building to save the effigy of Lady Godiva's Peeping Tom. Richard Keverne reported:

> The inn itself came into the front line for the first time in its life. In the days of the London blitz, I remember everybody commenting on the tendency for the bombs to single out churches and inns. The bombs were, in fact, quite indiscriminate. But because the church and the inn were the symbols of community life, their destruction was more noticeable.

Almost every city suffered. 'The old inns and houses in the neighbourhood of St Peter's have gone and the delight of artists is no more,' reflected a saddened C F W Dening in his fourth edition of *Old Inns of Bristol,* published in 1949. Among those blasted to the ground in the West Country port were the famous **Montague** at Kingsdown, **Hope and Anchor** on Redcliff Hill, **Bank Tavern** in Dolphin Street and the **Lamb and Flag** and **Bacchus Tavern** both in Temple Street. Another doomed historic hostelry was **The Raven** in St Mary-le-Port Street, 'a thoroughfare blitzed to such an extent that it is now lost.' Ironically the Bristol authorities beat Hitler's bombers to one of the wonders of the city in the same street – the medieval half-timbered **Swan** with its overhanging carved gables – which had been demolished to make way for an office block in 1936. The bombers destroyed the modern premises.

It is a condition of the licence, we understand, that a hostelry must remain open during structural alterations.

BUILDING TRADE: Brewers were worried that a pub closed because of war damage might lose its licence – so every effort was made to keep open, though not quite to this extent.

Groves & Whitnall estimated that about half their pubs in the built-up areas of Manchester had been severely damaged, with 215 licensed premises affected and 12 wiped completely off the streets. And it was not only the towns and cities which were struck from the air.

Theakston's Brewery in the remote country calm of Masham in North Yorkshire lost its brewery tap, the **White Bear Inn**, when a stray bomber dropped a stick of bombs on a terrace of houses, including the pub, killing many people. The licence was transferred to another building near the brewery's offices and the **White Bear** roared again.

By the end of 1941 it was estimated that the total number of licensed premises destroyed in Britain was 1,116, made up of 916 pubs and 200 off-licences. The value of these premises was put at £5,500,000 – and their licences were in legal jeopardy.

The brewers knew that under a strict interpretation of the law the renewal of the licences of damaged houses could be refused. According to a note in *Paterson*, the licensing law bible, 'Dilapidated premises requiring structural repair as distinct from decorative repair would be a good ground for refusal.' Most licensing benches, however, recognised that the war had brought exceptional conditions and generally renewed the licences of closed pubs. But the trade was uneasy, feeling naked without the comforting cloak of legal protection.

The Brewers' Journal reflected this suspicion in July 1941:
What is going on behind the scenes in regard to destroyed licensed premises at Birmingham, Coventry, Bristol and London where already representatives of the Government are preparing general plans for rebuilding destroyed areas? Our disquiet in this matter tends to increase as month by month there is withheld from the trade the right of licence revival given it in the last war. We say again: Give us back the security of our licences first; then, if you must, talk about their ultimate disposition.

In January 1942, the Home Secretary, Herbert Morrison, moved to remove this mounting anxiety. In response to a question in the House of Commons about the future of destroyed pubs, he replied:
It is recognised that it would not be right to allow the licences in these cases to lapse, and it seems clear that an amendment of the law is required to insure that they are kept alive. It is the intention of the Government to introduce the necessary legislation.

This promise was put into effect in the War Damage (Amendment) Bill. Brewery directors breathed a long sigh of relief. The legislation was vital. By 1944, it was estimated that 3,000 pubs had been boarded up or burnt down.

The licences might be kept alive – but no-one could bring back those who died in the ruins. Tales of landlords battling against the odds filled the press and helped maintain morale. Some grimmer stories had the censor reaching for the red pencil.

On 16 April, 1941, **The California** in Sutton, Surrey, took a direct hit, killing ten people. Though there was a human story of heroism for the newspapers to report the next day. Six-foot-six Canadian Jonathan Gibb had just stepped off a bus when the bar exploded. He held up a beam for three hours to prevent debris falling on a woman until she could be rescued.

BURIED ALIVE: Rescuers bring out one of the few to survive the bombing of The **Marples Hotel** in Sheffield in which 70 people died.

In one swift daylight raid on Hastings in May 1943, two Whitbread pubs, **The Warriors' Gate** and **The Swan**, were completely destroyed in two minutes, the licensee's family at **The Swan** all being killed along with many of the 40 Sunday lunchtime customers.

Sheffield suffered one of the worst pub incidents of the war. The grand **Marples Hotel** on the corner of Fitzalan Square and the High Street was struck by a heavy high-explosive bomb just before midnight on 12 December, 1940. It was the night of one of the worst air-raids of the war in South Yorkshire and nearly 80 people were sheltering in the cellar of the John Smith's house, some already wounded. The direct hit brought the whole seven-storey building crashing down into the basement. The ruin blazed all night. The next day seven people were rescued alive from the bottling store next to the main cellar. The rest had perished. It took 12 days to dig 64 bodies out of the rubble. The fragments of six or seven more brought the death total to around 70.

Fortunately such major disasters were rare, but tragedies on a smaller scale were common. The despair and harsh reality is brought out in this account of the **Carlton Tavern** in Kentish Town by the married daughter of the licensee, after the London pub was struck by a flying bomb.

We used to sleep in the cellar at one time during the war, but started sleeping upstairs again during a lull. We were in our beds when the bomb dropped and we were very lucky to escape injury. We were trapped in our rooms covered in debris until we were rescued and then had to go down on our

SAFE BELOW:
A landlord and his
family settle down
among the barrels for
a night in the cellar.

backsides and feel our way as it was a dark November night.
I pulled my son from his shattered cot which had a big boulder
resting on it. He was 14 months at the time.

My husband I left trying to sort himself out. I forgot about
him until an hour later when someone asked me where he
was. My father gave us a drink from a few bottles that were
left after they found my husband. My father got drunk later
and that was how our area manager found him. He said he
would have done the same although he was a teetotaller.
People tried to loot it, but there were too many people about
as they had made the pub the mortuary. There were quite a
number of our customers killed in the little houses opposite,
which was very upsetting as relatives arrived for news.

The **Carlton** was a Whitbread house and shortly after the war, in
a feature headlined 'The War Years in Retrospect,' the company's
house magazine commented in an article which could have applied
to all bombarded towns:

It is to the licensees of London that the major tribute is due.
We are too near the event to attempt a proper valuation of
their services to the community. Let us hope that one day in
the history books they will get their due reward of praise.
Throughout the bombing they stuck to their posts with a
constancy, fortitude and unselfishness and cheerfulness that
were an example to all.

In these testing days the retail trade achieved a new stature.

To many thousands of bombed and nerve-worn Londoners, the public house offered a welcome respite from the pandemonium outside and overhead. It was one of the few remaining sources of comfort and encouragement on which they could always depend.

L A G Strong in his history of Charrington's summed up the role of the landlord in wartime:

A specially memorable feature in all this misfortune was the gallantry and determination of the licensees. No matter what the damage, they were united in a determination to stay open somehow. Surveyors and builders helped to prop up and save the damaged buildings, so that the weary customers could get their beer; and there is no doubt in the minds of all but a prejudiced minority that this has helped as much as any other single factor to maintain the people's morale and keep them relaxed and cheerful.

When Canterbury was heavily blitzed in 1942, Mackeson's lorries from Hythe were the only ones on the scene the next morning, supplying their houses through the ruined streets. The brewery had decided to make a deliberate gesture of support, even though it was not Canterbury's day for deliveries. Head Brewer John Wilmot recalled:

We received at Hythe some weeks afterwards a letter from the Canterbury police saying it was noticed we were the only brewery to supply Canterbury that day, and that it was much appreciated by all the populace. The heartening sight of seeing a brewer's drayman making normal deliveries was most cheering.

It was not, of course, just civilians who appreciated the pub. In the bars gathered soldiers and sailors before setting off on dangerous missions. And it was one of the first places they headed to when home on leave. Here the Local Defence Volunteers, later the Home Guard, met to watch and wait. Above all, the famous 'few' found the pub an ideal place to relax after risking their lives in the skies.

'You begin to long for a glass of beer,' said Squadron Leader J A Leathart, when describing a dog-fight for the Press in London in August 1940, at the height of the Battle of Britain:

The first thing you know is a noise rather like a typewriter, but much more deadly – a Messerschmitt 109 firing from behind. You shake him off, climb high and then spiral down until you see a nice juicy-looking German fighter. You descend upon him and after a few aerobatics one of you goes down.

It gets very hot in the cockpit, and you begin to long for a glass of beer. Eventually, when you have dispersed the enemy and with luck brought down many of them, you reach home, and there at last is a sparkling glass of beer awaiting you.

Air Vice Marshal Sir Cecil Bouchier, commander of the Hornchurch Fighter Section, echoed this view from the cockpit:

I remember how the chaps [the pilots] used to flock up to the mess at the end of each day's fighting, flop down on the hall floor, just as they were, straight from their aircraft, and call for their beer.

This was their one great relaxation, the beer they had dreamt about all day. No-one drank anything but draught beer and mighty good stuff it was, food and drink to the tired and thirsty. Often a leader bringing his squadron home, fearful of being late, would radio from halfway across the Channel – 'Keep the bar open, we'll be down in 20 minutes.'

Many squadrons did not have their own bars or preferred the comfort of the pub. The Malling aerodrome in Kent was secretly fitted with specially-trained night fighter squadrons to counter the enemy's attacks after dark. Air ace Guy Gibson wrote in his book *Enemy Coast Ahead*: 'That first night we stood by but the weather was bad and group released the squadron about nine. Down to the **Startled Saint** we went to sample the beer; it was good and everyone was happy.'

The airfield ran right alongside Leney's Wateringbury Brewery. Managing Director John Marchant later recalled:

We sighed, prayed and watched as our pilots time after time left us, took off, fought for us against odds in great wheeling circles just above and then – if lucky – came back to us with some nonchalant quip about someone having pinched the pint he'd started.

The brewery regularly entertained the airmen. 'True it is that many, when calling on us to see how it's made, seemed less interested in the process than the finished product. They were none the less welcome for that!'

Not all breweries were quite so happy to have airfields in their neighbourhood. The Air Ministry could always pull rank. When Great Staughton airfield was extended, two pubs belonging to Wells & Winch of Biggleswade in Bedfordshire – **The Dolphin** at Great Staughton and the **Bushel and Strike** at Staughton Moor – were demolished to make way for the new landing strip.

SIGNING OFF: The names of many fighter pilots from the Battle of Britain were scrawled on a blackboard at the **White Hart** in Brasted in Kent.

Some pubs were celebrated for their close airforce connections. The **White Hart** at Brasted, between Sevenoaks and Westerham, was the favourite watering hole of pilots from nearby Biggin Hill airfield. Many famous names scrawled their signatures on the black-out screen in the bar. After the war the screen was framed and in December 1946, was officially unveiled by one of those who had left their mark and survived, Group Captain Malan, as a memorial to 'the few'.

Airmen also left their names on the walls of the historic **Swan** at Lavenham in Suffolk. 'These signatures are still preserved,' recorded A W Coysh in *Historic English Inns* in 1972. 'So is the half-gallon glass boot they used for competitive drinking. The record swig is said to have taken a mere 22 seconds.'

Many bomber crews crowded into pubs in and around York, some engraving their names on a mirror in **Betty's Bar**, which was then popularly known as **The Dive**, in St Helen's Square close to the Minster. **The Blacksmith's Arms** at Seaton Ross near York is still known by its war-time name of **The Bombers** as it was packed with flyers from nearby Melbourne Airfield. For Canadians, Australians and many other nationalities, it became a home from home.

When the Americans entered the war they also entered Britain's pubs. The American authorities realised that for most of their men this would be a step into the unknown. In their official booklet issued to all units going to Britain, they warned:

> The British have theatres and movies – which they call cinemas – as we do; but the great place of recreation is the tavern. The usual drink is beer, which is not an imitation of German beer as our beer is, but ale (but they usually call it beer or bitter). The British are beer drinkers and can 'hold it'. Beer is now below peace-time strength, but can still make a man's tongue wag at both ends. You will be welcome in British taverns as long as you remember one thing – the inn or tavern is the poor man's club or gathering place where men have come to see their friends not strangers.

KEEPING UP APPEARANCES: Ignoring the havoc around her, a woman scrubs the steps of a pub at the Elephant and Castle while workmen repair a huge bomb crater in the road (*Courage Archive*).

Broadcaster Ed Morrow, who had lived in London for some years, advised his fellow countrymen that if when they walked in the conversation stopped, to take no notice. 'They would do that anyway if an Englishman came in who lived in a village five miles away.' His advice was: 'Join in the chat and stand your round if it seems to be your turn. But don't jingle your money or think that by buying drinks all round you will gain popularity.' Finally, he warned that it was not clever to drink too much.

The Brewers' Journal was also preparing the trade for the invasion. 'The Yanks are coming; they are here,' the magazine reported in August 1942:

In ever-increasing numbers they will occupy our countryside ... and filter into our villages and towns when off duty or on leave. We are a shy people – arrogance does not account for our standoffishness – and are perhaps not good mixers. No nation has closer friends or fewer acquaintances than the English. Many of our fighting cousins will be welcome into our homes; thousands will find warm-hearted hospitality in the village inn and town pub.

The mine hosts of our hostelries should be on the look-out for United States servicemen and give them the welcome they deserve. As representatives of a younger world they will be found to be both resourceful and independent. But all of them are far from home and kindly, unostentatious concern for their welfare will not be misunderstood.

The pub was where the new allies met. Mr R A Bray, chairman of the Surrey Public House Trust, said that the men from overseas believed they have learned more about the British through friendly associations in the bars of Britain than from any other experiences. This filtered right to the top. General Patten stayed at **The Bells** of Peover in Lower Peover, Cheshire. General Eisenhower also enjoyed a glass there along with many officers of the American army stationed nearby.

A few pubs had to compromise their English traditions. The courtyard of the old coaching inn, **The George** in Huntingdon, was taken over by an American doughnut bakery.

Some pubs were even more directly involved in the war. **The Bell** at Sandwich, Kent, had an anti-tank gun installed in one of its bathrooms. Radar experts homed in on the **Crown and Castle** at Orford in Suffolk. Others gained grander status. The imposing **White Hart** at Salisbury for a while served as the headquarters of Southern Command. While the walls of the **Royal Hotel** at Bideford, Devon, and the **Golden Lion** at Southwick, Hampshire, protected many of the secrets of the D-Day landings in Normandy.

But it was as the community's citadel that the pub really earned its spurs during the crisis years of war.

OFF TO WORK: Many licensees had other jobs like Jack Cliffe of **The Waggoners**, near London, who is seen off by his wife and customers as he goes to work as an observer, watching for enemy planes.

MIRACLE IN THE MASH TUN
Surmounting the Shortages

The bombs dropped the dreadful drama of war right into the homes and bars of Britain. But for most breweries, most of the time, the war was less dramatic. It was just a daily struggle to keep going.

The Government wanted to keep the public's pint pots full – but that did not mean the breweries escaped the mean realities of rationing and restrictions. As the conflict ground on many were scraping the bottom of the barrel for supplies and staff.

Yet by the end of the war, the amount of beer brewed had increased by a third, rising by eight million barrels from 24.7m in 1938 to 32.7m bulk barrels in 1945, the largest output since 1914. Given the circumstances, it was nothing short of a miracle, even if the magic of beer was somewhat watered down. The average strength of a pint fell from a gravity of just under 1041 to 1034.6, a drop of about 15 per cent. The Government demanded quantity rather than quality and most strong ales disappeared off the bars altogether.

The heart of beer is malted barley and the brewers scanned the grain fields anxiously as war broke out, particularly since the Government immediately banned the import of barley for brewing. If this embargo had been enforced a few years before, it could have been a catastrophe.

Many British brewers once routinely imported a large part of their barley requirements from as far afield as Australia and California

PRECIOUS CROP:
Barley was the heart of beer and once the war cut off imports it was in short supply, as this cartoon demonstrates.

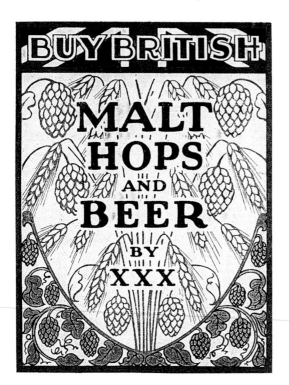

BUY BRITISH:
Fortunately, before 1939
the Brewers' Society's
'Beer is Best' campaign
included a 'Buy British'
slant which reduced the
need for imports.

where the strong sun produced better ripened crops. From the 1880s to 1914 between a quarter and a third of all barley was shipped in. This pattern of trade was dented in the First World War but then revived strongly. In 1932 out of 475,000 tons of barley malted in Britain, only 280,000 were home-grown. Nearly 40 per cent was imported. Reflecting this decline in demand, farmers switched to other crops, the acreage under barley in Britain declining from 2.2 million in 1880 to 750,000 in 1933. If the British Isles had been isolated then, the national glass of beer would soon have been little more than half full.

However, in an attempt to help lift the depressed economy the brewers pledged in 1933 to buy as much home-grown barley as possible in return for a reduction in excise duty. The 'Beer is Best' campaign launched that year by the Brewers' Society also contained a 'British is Best' element. The flag was waved above the froth and when the Second World War broke out Britain was in a better position to meet its own needs. In 1935 the brewers agreed to buy at least 7.5 million hundredweight of British barley. By 1939 purchases had swelled to 9.5 million with imports down to 23 per cent.

With imports banned, British farmers, who had once complained bitterly about the brewers' habit of buying abroad, were now firmly in the tractor seat. Unlike many foodstuffs, the cost of malting barley was not at first restricted. Prices almost doubled in the first year of war from around 30s a quarter to an average of 58s 7d. Farmers rushed to grow the new cash crop with the acreage under barley expanding rapidly, doubling in size during the war.

Possible malt substitutes like imported maize grits and flakes were running out by early 1940. Rice soon followed. The sugar allocation for brewing was cut by 30 per cent in April that year. The Government's only restriction on how much could be brewed was that the overall amount must not exceed the standard barrelage for 1939. Permits for this were issued by the Ministry of Food and supplies were eagerly snapped up. Brewers were not allowed to stockpile and carry over malt to the next season. So they had to rush to the market once supplies were available. Barley growers could name their price.

In the summer of 1941 a meeting between the National Farmers' Union and the Brewers' Society broke up in disagreement, with the brewers not prepared to accept a maximum price of 115s a quarter. They felt this was unreasonably high. But by the time the Government, alarmed at the escalating cost of barley, stepped in the following year, the price had shot up again. The maximum figure was fixed at 140 shillings a quarter in July 1942.

Though unhappy, the brewers bit their lips and kept quiet. At least the high prices ensured more malting barley was produced – and none was sold off cheaply as animal fodder as the temperance activists demanded. The following year the maximum price for malting barley fell back to 110s a quarter.

The supplies were spun out by two agreements with the Government. In February 1941 the brewers voluntarily agreed to reduce the average gravity of their beers by 10 per cent. That way the same amount of malt could produce more – but weaker – beer. In January 1942 this was reduced by a further 5 per cent, except where a brewer's average gravity was already below 1030.

Some brewers like Wilsons of Manchester still managed to retain a respectable strength as their beers had quite high gravities to start with. Their average gravity dropped from 1043.3 in 1939 to 1039 in 1941 and 1036.8 in 1942. Others fell into the near-beer category. The average gravity of Steward & Patteson of Norwich in 1942 was 1031.1, with their weakest Light Bitter and XX at 1026. Another East Anglian brewer, Greene King of Bury St Edmunds in neighbouring Suffolk, was by 1943 producing just one beer, in light and dark versions, with a diluted gravity of 1027. These were so weak they would not have been banned in America during Prohibition.

The Minister of Food, Lord Woolton, knew what he was doing. At a trade lunch in London in March 1943, he arrived late and jokingly remarked: 'I am glad to see you are all sober,' adding with a mischievous twinkle, 'I knew you would be. We have so managed the beer problem in this war that you always know that people are going to be sober. We have got a very good beer – one which cannot do anyone any harm!'

Not all brewers beamed broadly at these pleasantries. Some worried about what was happening to the national beverage. It was not just Government requests and the shortage of brewing materials which were driving the strength of beer down. The three hefty rises in duty in the first year of war also encouraged brewers to produce lower gravity beers which attracted less tax. Then there was the question of the customer's pocket, as the worried author of the brewing notes in *The Brewers' Journal* pointed out in February 1941.

During the few opportunities for contemplation that occur in these times, some of us are finding ourselves wondering what is going to become of the quality of our national beverage in days to come . . . because of the fantastic heights to which taxation has soared and correspondingly fantastic depths to which average gravities have consequently fallen.

With regard to the bulk of the draught beer consumed up and down the country there is no point in hiding from ourselves the fact that much of it has to be brought within the purse of those whose incomes are still of pre-war magnitude and who, if they are not to give up drinking altogether, must confine themselves to the consumption of the cheapest (and therefore weakest) pint available.

This tendency, the result of the cumulative effect of two successive wars, has completely changed the character of the national drink. Although there is much to be said, on the grounds of sobriety, for the disappearance of the heavy beers of pre-1914 days, the technical brewer cannot but view with apprehension and discomfiture the possibility that the average gravity of British beer may well become established at little above the technically minimal gravity – a gravity at which he can feel little pride in his product and at which the exercise of his art is at a discount.

Surely it is not beyond the intelligence to devise some method whereby reasonable taxation can be imposed without the apparently inevitable debasement of the national drink of our people.

In January 1942 *The Brewers' Journal* warned the Government that 'they should beware of giving to the workers beer of a quality which – if the reduction in gravities is further pursued – might lead to its being unacceptable.' This leading article concluded: 'In this war we do not wish the public to attach to the lowest-priced beer the gibe which gained currency in the last war, when it was contumaciously referred to as "Government ale". Beer must be allowed to retain its dignity.'

According to journalists at a press conference in August 1941, beer had already lost its dignity. An official of the Ministry of Food was told by one newspaperman that 'the quality of beer sold today is terrible.' His colleagues agreed. But a leading brewer touring the country that summer was surprised to discover how full-bodied were many of the reduced gravity brews: 'One of the outstanding features of many of the beers tasted has been the remarkable palate fullness they have possessed, considering that in many cases they were of modest gravity.' Many brewers were managing to mask the weakness of their ales. He felt they had gone 'a long way towards satisfying the consumer that the beer is not watery, and that is something in these days.'

The position at least was not as bad as during the First World War, when the average gravity of beer sank to 1030 in 1919. In the Second World War the average gravity hovered around the 1035 mark. Lord Woolton was proud of the achievement. He told the House of Lords in May 1942:

Some 25 years ago many people begged and prayed for a light drink which the working people might have, and which would give them pleasure and satisfaction without the evils of excessive drinking. We have that beer now; people are enjoying it and it is doing them very little harm. I believe that this policy has met with the approval of the country.

The Brewers' Journal believed the country's attitude depended on their age group.

There is a section of the public comprising mainly the older generation of men who deplore the lack of strength in the national beverage as it reaches them today. The younger generation, including members of the Forces, seem to have few complaints on this score. To them, engaged as they are for the most part in hard physical work, beer is looked upon as a thirst-quencher (and the beer of today fulfils this role even better than the pre-war stronger beers) and the drinking of it as a social act.

Besides diluting the people's pint, the Minister of Food also urged brewers to use other materials in the mash tun where possible. Barley flakes produced by steam treatment and rolling were provided in 1942 to conserve malt supplies. Brewers in some parts of the country were alarmed to discover that they would only receive beet sugar – without any chance to experiment with its effects. Lactose was banned for brewing purposes. But the most controversial move was an attempt to introduce oats.

In January 1943 the Ministry requested that the industry further reduce its consumption of barley by 10 per cent – the Government wanted to use the cereal for making bread – and replace the lost barley malt with flaked or malted oats. 'A strong recommendation was issued by the society to all brewers ... experiments were made and by July the target of 10 per cent saving in barley had for practical purposes been reached,' recorded the Brewers' Society's Annual Report for 1943. But not all brewers had complied. Not everyone wanted their oats.

The columnist 'Brettanomyces' in The Brewers' Journal reflected the reservations of many brewers when he began his brewing notes about oats in May 1943 with the provocative quotation that they were 'The food of horses in England and men in Scotland.' He said oats had 'become the burning topic of the day.'

'The use of oats will no doubt raise fresh problems to harass the war-time brewer.' He pointed out that oats were 'low in starch and other extract-producing materials' and 'in view of the low gravities now prevailing, may result in insufficient yeast food.' 10 per cent of barley malt in the mash tun would have to be replaced by 15 per cent oats because of the much poorer extract. He worried that oats would cripple robust yeasts. 'Yeast, like most micro-organisms, may go on for some time without showing any starvation effect, and then suddenly deterioration may set in.'

Some brewers were more forthright in their views. Captain W N R Garne of Garne's Burford Brewery in Oxfordshire wrote to the Brewers' Society in May 1943 after receiving the circular about using oats:

We again confirm our decision that it is quite impossible for

us to use oat malt in the brewing of our beers at this brewery
. . . I am the practical brewer (have been brewing here for 40
years) and know what can be done and what cannot be done,
and I will give up my job rather than be persuaded to do the
wrong thing.

We want to win this war and win it as quickly as possible.
We contend that 'war beer' is bad enough without making it
worse. Two pints of good beer are better for a manual worker
than three pints of indifferent.

The argument that 'most of the brewers in this country are
already using oats' leaves me cold. I cannot and will not spoil
good materials, neither have I the time to get into more
difficulties for it just does NOT help win the war.

That brewers will get into difficulties owing to the use of
oats is admitted by your circular dated April 15. The offer of
help you so casually make is not attractive. No brewer, unless
he is a fool, who has ever been though the nightmare of returns
(beer sent back from the pub), would look for, invite and court
trouble with his beers with his eyes open, when scores of other
difficulties have to be met and overcome every day.

Captain Garne was already upset by the forced changes the war
had brought to his beers in this quiet corner of the Cotswolds, where
Garne's owned a handful of pubs.

Since the war we have had to entirely discontinue the brewing
of an all-malt (English) beer, 1055 gravity, which was a
backbone to our yeast. For over 80 years we have never had
to have a change of yeast. Our beers felt the absence of such a
yeast and very great care and attention has had to be given
whilst suffering this change to avoid trouble and keep the
character of our beers.

Further our Bitter and Mild beers have suffered still further
changes and trials through the lowering of gravities and the
compulsory restriction of sugar and the consequent use of
substitutes – a word absolutely foreign to our beers and
brewery before the war.

The eventual effect on the yeast of using oats in the mash
tun is an entirely unknown quantity, even to your 'experts'. I
certainly cannot waste the material or spare the time to work
out so risky an experiment in these days under present
conditions in this brewery.

Lord Woolton has played hell with the quality of beer to

get quantity, but are the public going to remain satisfied with the product? The tendency of oats to produce a more bitter and drier flavour to an already weak beer is absolutely out of place. The public, particularly the man who sweats as he works, wants sweetness. He requires it.

My brewer was taken over three years ago, 24 of our employees have gone since. Despite this we have kept up a maximum output of beer, to say nothing of a large wine and spirit trade. Last year we contributed over £30,000 in taxes, a fact of which I am proud. All this has been done because I have worked 10 hours a day, done all night work involving paying visits to the brewery at 3am and 5am three nights a week for three years. My holidays have been nine days – three days each – for the three years.

If you or the Ministry of Food expect me to take on fresh difficulties, then I shall certainly seek another job where my efforts will help the war effort and I shall not be b...... about – excuse my expression – by those who have no conception of the practical working out of the rules and regulations they make from office stools.

My age is 57 and I am suffering 37 per cent disability from the last war, but despite this I do my duty as a Home Guard in addition to my long and continuous working hours.

Perhaps Captain Garne's message got through. In October Lord Woolton, after expressing his appreciation that the brewers had 'substantially' implemented his request to replace 10 per cent of their barley with oats, asked them to reverse this policy. He said that following a good harvest there was now an ample supply of barley, while oats were in short supply. But perhaps he had learnt that burdening brewers with oats had been the last straw.

Certainly another maverick of the mash tun – potatoes – was never seriously pursued. The Brewers' Society's Annual Report for 1943 noted that 'experiments with the use of potatoes continued, and potatoes in the form of flakes or flour have been used by certain breweries to a very small extent.'

Those brewers who were asked to try chips with everything were far from impressed. Greene King of Suffolk found that dried potatoes gave customers terrible wind, and managing director Major Lake congratulated his employees in 1942 for producing 'a satisfactory article out of the worst brewing materials I have ever experienced.'

Guinness's massive and modern Park Royal Brewery in London

boasted a miniature brewery in its laboratory, just completed before war broke out. This trial plant was asked to test many potential replacements for barley. Technical director Dr John Webb recorded:

There was only one adjunct which we were unable to use, namely kibbled potatoes which consisted of dried potato slices produced by the sugar beet factories during their close season. The Extra Stout brewed with this material tasted strongly of potatoes; consequently we had to abandon its use, but we found that flaked rye and flaked oats were satisfactory.

The Brewers' Journal wearily hoped in July 1943 that 'the thought that beer can be made from just anything' is 'not taken too seriously by government departments.' The magazine had heard that

... the question of the disposal of a possible surplus of potatoes is receiving the attention of the Food Ministry, and the ministry has asked its scientific advisers to consult with Professor Hopkins of Birmingham (college of brewing) to see whether and to what extent potatoes can be used in the production of beer.

A logical member of the brewing profession may observe that this is only to be expected, since the brewers have already absorbed what seemed to be a surplus of oats, and the more frivolous may horrify the more serious by speculations as to the likely course of events in the case of a sudden fall in the pig population accompanied by an embarrassing increase in the contents of the pig garbage bins.

The magazine added:

It is now well over two years since private enterprise produced potato flakes, and some brewers supported it by trying them out in the brewery. They were not very successful . . . there are limitations to the materials that can be used for producing a silk purse.

The brewers were tiring of testing ever stranger adjuncts and the Government ceased to press spuds and the like after 1943. They realised the importance of maintaining the reputation of an already seriously weakened product.

This was particularly important at a time when the keeping quality of beer was also under threat. That other vital ingredient of a good glass – hops – was also in short supply. Hops were not only important for flavour, imparting bitterness and aroma, but also acted as a vital preservative, stopping the beer going sour.

Like barley, imports were banned at the beginning of the war, so brewers had to rely entirely on the home supply. Unlike barley, it was not a crop which could be easily or quickly grown on new ground to meet extra demand. Hops were produced in two main areas – Kent and Worcestershire – and the acreage had halved since 1914 from 37,000 to 18,000.

The hop fields were tightly bound in regulations and restrictions, even in peace-time, with set prices and production quotas. Sales and marketing were complex processes. This specialist arm of agriculture was not geared up to meet the sudden demands of war. In 1940 there were even doubts if the crop could be picked. The farmers relied on families from the East End of London coming out into the fields at harvest time; many were reluctant that summer to enter the cockpit county of Kent where Hitler's troops were expected at any moment.

The *Brewing Trade Review* reported in October 1940:

There was only a week or two back, considerable doubt whether more than a portion of the hop crop could be picked owing to the difficulty of getting enough pickers to enter the danger zones of Kent and Sussex. It is, however, an ill wind that blows nobody any good, and one of the effects of the recent large-scale bombing attacks on London has been a sudden change of attitude on the part of those who normally spend their holidays picking hops, who have flocked to the gardens as a refuge from their bombed neighbourhoods.

The Luftwaffe may have saved the hop crop on this occasion, but within weeks they almost destroyed it. Under the archaic sales system for hops, virtually the whole crop from Kent was funnelled into a tiny area in the Borough of Southwark in London and packed into a few warehouses. The Government

STIFF UPPER LIP: By 1944 many had become used to aerial attacks. The caption for this cartoon from 'Time to Laugh' magazine read: 'My dear sir, this is nothing! You should have been here in 1940.'

realised the danger and wanted stocks to go directly from the farms to the breweries, but lack of storage space on the farms and a reluctance to change time-honoured traditions meant most of the valuable hop-pockets filed like a funeral procession into Southwark. The inevitable happened. The bulging buildings were bombed and a fifth of the crop was lost.

The heavy losses meant the Brewers' Society had to redistribute stocks, more than 9,000 pockets being transferred between brewers. A new distribution scheme was belatedly introduced for 1941 with hops being graded on the farms or in small country warehouses, before being sent straight to the breweries. The use of the Borough for any large quantity of hops was banned. The Ministry of Food ordered that beer hopping rates be reduced by 20 per cent to help spin out supplies. In 1941 brewers still only received three-quarters of the hops they wanted and the bitter problem only appeared to fade by 1943 when brewers received 95 per cent of their contracts.

But many brewers had been partly surviving on old stocks held before the conflict. As the war dragged on shortages became more acute again. Imports before the war had accounted for 17.5 per cent of the market and their absence was keenly felt as British growers could not make up the deficit. Only in 1943 did the Government allow an extra 2,000 acres to be planted with hops and as it took three seasons before a full crop was obtained this had no immediate effect, particularly since farmers did not rush to take up the option, which required long-term investment.

The hops committee of the Brewers' Society reported in 1945: 'The position has now been reached when brewers' stocks are exhausted and the majority will have used up all their hops by the beginning of November and will be dependent entirely upon the arrival of 1945 hops to maintain their beer output.' Brewing was only continuing on a hand to mouth basis, with rare varieties like Goldings speeding straight from the hop gardens to the boiling coppers in the breweries.

The industry was even scouring the newly-liberated lands of Europe for supplies. 'Every effort is being made with the help of the Ministry of Food to find supplies of hops in Continental countries to ease the present shortage.' An increasing number of frustrated brewers began to consider growing their own. Shepherd Neame of Faversham in the hop county of Kent bought their own hop farm, Queen Court at Ospringe, in 1944. Only after repeated pleadings did the Government eventually give permission for the import of hop concentrate from America.

As the war ended the brewers were only a few hops ahead of a major crisis. The Brewers' Society rushed to gain import licences to buy 30,000 hundredweight of hops from Czechoslovakia, Yugoslavia and the American zone of Germany.

While the brewers desperately eked out their limited supplies, everyone knew this was not their major anxiety. At least those who were left knew it. For the commodity in shortest supply was staff.

Brewing was not one of the most labour intensive industries. It did not need many hands to make light ale. But it did need skilled staff to work efficiently, and many of these workers were soon drafted away. From the boardroom to the cellars men were on the march out of the gates.

One of the reasons why the industry was so heavily hit was that in many breweries military men issued the orders. Colonel This and Major That were familiar figures on many brewery boards. This strong service connection meant that a large number of breweries

MARCHING OUT: The eagerness of many breweries to set up military units meant they lost many men. Fortunately for Mitchell's and Butler's of Birmingham, this fine body of men were their ARP unit – and stayed at home at their Cape Hill Brewery (*Bass Museum*).

had led the way in developing Territorial Army units before the war. 'The result was that when hostilities began breweries all over the country lost many of their best men,' reported the *Brewing Trade Review* in May 1940. Some were cut to the bone.

William Hancock's of Cardiff and Swansea was ruled by a succession of Colonel Gaskells. The board's enthusiastic recruitment for the Territorial Army meant that production almost came to a standstill when the Territorials were called up. Troops of men filed out of the two breweries in South Wales. It was a story repeated across Britain. At Wells & Winch in Bedfordshire a large number of men left the Biggleswade brewery to man 'A' battery of the 52nd Regiment of the Royal Artillery in France under director Major J A Redman.

The Military Service Act meant more men were enlisted. Only key figures like brewers, aged over 30, were exempt. Many brewery workforces were seriously depleted. Colonel Serocold told Watney's first war-time AGM in August 1940 that in every department 'we have had serious depletions of strength; upwards of 50 men of our staff and upwards of 300 of our employees are on service, so that you can imagine that things have not been altogether easy in working the brewery.' A year later the numbers had considerably increased with 112 staff and 509 workmen now called away.

In smaller breweries the loss of a lesser number of men was often more severely felt as there were fewer left to bear the burden. The position was even worse in the maltings, where skilled men were needed to turn the malt on the huge floors. When the Chairman of the Brewers' Society, Sir Richard Wells, was asked at the end of 1941 what concerned him most about the future, he replied: 'The greatest reason for misgiving is the severe shortage of labour in the maltings.' Without a steady supply of malt the breweries would be crippled.

In October that year the *Brewing Trade Review* commented:
The steady drain of men of military age has brought the brewing industry down to a point where the greatest difficulty is being experienced in carrying on the production and distribution of beer, and in some instances is the ruling factor which governs local shortages. Even more important is the effect of this drainage of manpower from maltings, which has brought about a most serious diminution in the malting capacity of the country as a whole. . . . It is not far out to say that the loss of one skilled floorman will reduce the potential output of malt by a thousand quarters in a season.
The answer to the manpower problem, once the pool of unem-

BOTTLING GIRLS: Women had already taken over one area of the brewery before the war – working on the bottling lines like this one at George's in Bristol (*Courage Archive*).

ployed men was drained, was to employ boys, pensioners – and above all women. When Whitbread looked back at the war years, the London brewery recalled: 'The shortage of labour was perhaps our most pressing problem. Old employees were recalled from retirement and the services of women had to be recruited, the latter at one time representing 20 per cent of the total number of employees.'

Women had already gained a considerable foothold in breweries before the war, working on the growing number of bottling lines. But now they expanded into other areas. Even Guinness at Park Royal, which brought over a number of neutral Irishmen to London to plug the gaps, found it necessary to employ women in jobs previously regarded as men's work. The stout company later remembered:

When in 1940 women were employed in several departments, even the most diehard of the old brigade were mollified by the necessity of the job they were doing and by the efficient way in which they did it. Soon only visitors from St James's Gate [Guinness's Dublin brewery] were surprised to see blonde heads bobbing over the sides of skimmers, manicured

HEAVY WORK: Women now rolled into new areas like handling heavy casks at Watney's Stag Brewery (*Courage Archive*).

hands ramming huge pockets of hops into coppers and trim figures deftly manoeuvring casks about the bank.

The idea of women moving huge, heavy barrels would have been unthinkable before the war, but they soon mastered the tricks of the trade. 'The women quickly learned the technique of using the shape of the cask to move and up-end them to reduce physical effort,' recalled administration manager Tom Styles. They also adopted the appropriate footwear. 'They rejected wellington boots for the old-fashioned clogs to keep their feet warm and dry, and soon adopted the rolling gait of all clog wearers.'

Soon the only concern about women was whether they would follow the men into the services. Their work was highly valued. In 1941 one radio commentator declared that 'efforts must be made to get feminine labour away from breweries for work of greater importance.' Later in the war increasing numbers were called into the armed forces, civil defence or enlisted for munition work.

Staff continued to haemorrhage and by the end of the conflict desperate measures were called for. Wells & Winch brought in Italian prisoners of war from a nearby camp to carry out general labouring work.

Women also took over running many of Britain's pubs as their husbands were called up. Girls were wanted more than ever to man the bars. Some gained equality of pay. One advert for three barmaids read: 'Men's wages will be given to efficient girls.' In Glasgow the hard-line council had to relax its 30-year rule banning barmaids as half of the city's barmen had been called up.

The Brewers' Journal commented in February 1941: 'It is quite clear that the licensed houses of the country have to a very large extent now to be carried on by women, and this will become more marked in the future.'

Another major headache for breweries was transport. Brewing beer was no use if it could not reach the customer. Yet almost overnight many brewery lorries vanished. Half of Charrington's fleet in London was commandeered for the army. And it was always the best vehicles which went to the front.

Prudent managers quickly bought second-hand lorries. But soon this required official permits. Extra vehicles were hired. Some brewers returned to the satisfying clip-clop of the dray horse for local deliveries to try and beat petrol rationing. Mann's Brewery in the East End of London built its four-footed fleet up to 130 horses during the war.

When the conflict broke out many customers went to great lengths to safeguard their supplies. H Westwell & Sons of Rhos-on-Sea in North Wales sent their lorry all the way to London to pick up a load of beer, as Watney's *Red Barrel* magazine of October 1939 revealed:

> They left Llandudno at nine o'clock on the Sunday morning and got as far as London Colney by five o'clock Sunday afternoon, where they found it difficult to obtain sleeping accommodation. They arrived at the Stag Brewery at 8 o'clock on Monday morning, deposited their empties and obtained a load of milk stout. They then went to Mortlake and picked up some pale ale and brown ale for bottling as well as container beers, leaving Mortlake about 4.30pm in the afternoon on their long return journey to North Wales, carrying in all approximately five tons of beer. Good work!

Such early initiatives were praised and widely copied. Watney's agents also journeyed up from as far afield as Devon and Cornwall, Liverpool and Fleetwood. 'Our Scottish agents, Messrs Dunn of Glasgow, were determined that the Scotsmen should not go without their milk stout, of which they are so fond, and they too sent their lorry down with empty casks and returned with a full load.' But soon such trips were seen as wasteful of fuel, time and manpower.

To head off the imposition of an official transport system, neighbouring breweries entered into agreements whereby they would deliver to each other's pubs if they were in their area, or exchange free trade business. A survey by the Brewers' Society in 1941 showed that 92 per cent of deliveries were within 30 miles of the brewery, the great bulk being within 15 miles. Soon this was improved through further rationalisation of trade. Most breweries delivered beer less frequently; a few investigated the use of gas as an alternative fuel for their lorries. Others swapped houses; Steward & Patteson of Norwich exchanged pubs with Lacons of Great Yarmouth in East Anglia in 1943.

The Brewers' Society waved the big stick at those reluctant to co-operate in this voluntary effort. 'The council emphasise that considerations of preserving goodwill can no longer be weighed against the imperative need to economise in transport,' stated the Annual Report in 1942. 'The process of cutting out wasteful journeys must be continued and accelerated.'

Despite improvements in efficiency, the Government was not satisfied. The Ministry of Food decided early in 1943 to place control of transport in the hands of its regional food officers, with the country divided into 88 zones. Long-distance deliveries, unless by ship or rail, were ruled out. Only two breweries – Bass and Guinness – were classified as national brewers and allowed to deliver their special beers across the country. A few others were designated distributive brewers and allowed broad distribution. Most were restricted to their heartland.

Many brewers muttered into their beer, but the system seems to have worked. A survey found that the same barrelage was delivered in 1943 as in 1941 but using 22 per cent less petrol through improved loading and shorter journeys. A growth of six per cent in barrelage between the years moved to the railways. Canals also flowed back into favour, their use by breweries increasing by 54 per cent by 1944. Guinness moved half their traffic from London to their Birmingham stores off the railways and onto barges despite the slower transit times.

The use of coastal shipping increased by 118 per cent – though not without some heavy losses. In December 1942 the SS *Lindisfarne* bound for Newcastle with 700 hogsheads of Guinness was sunk by the enemy. In April 1943 the SS *Dynamo* was lost with 1,085 hogsheads of stout of which 100 casks were recovered. William Younger of Edinburgh also suffered, losing four cargoes during the war. Fortunately the first two in 1941 were only carrying empty casks back to Leith from London. More seriously in 1945 *The Egholm* and *The Crightoun* were sunk while carrying full loads in the opposite direction. These were more than a few drops of beer in the ocean. *The Egholm*'s cargo was 33 hogsheads, 215 barrels, 311 kils, 264 firkins and 52 pins, besides 28 hogsheads and 50 kils of McEwan's for export to the military.

Another fuel problem was in the brewhouse itself where coal was needed to fire the boilers and coppers. The Ministry of Power insisted that no more than two weeks' worth of stocks should be held at the brewery and demanded better use of the black gold. Fuel efficiency committees raked over the ashes and many boilers were switched to coke. Good stoking coal was often in short supply. Simonds of Reading blamed their beer shortages in the summer of 1941 on the failure of the collieries to fulfil their contracts, as the coal had been diverted to other factories by the Mines Department.

In the pubs it also proved difficult to keep the home fires burning. At Chester's Brewery in Manchester they supplemented their supplies of coal and logs in the bar grate with some strange concoctions. 'Ovoids' – which were egg-shaped mixtures of coal dust and cement – were used to keep fires going, as were old aeroplane and car tyres cut to suitable sizes. 'These burned with an offensive smell and left the fireplaces full of reinforcing wires, but at least they gave a cheerful blaze and a house without a fire was a house without a customer,' recalled Frank Cowen, who worked for the brewery during the war.

When Hitler thrust deep into Poland in 1939, he cut British breweries off from one of their most important supplies. The industry depended on wooden casks for rolling out draught beer. Memel oak from the Baltic – strong, straight and supple – had been used for years to make wooden casks. It was the most suitable wood from which the coopers fashioned staves and barrel ends. Now the craftsmen of the carpenters' shop, once they had used up their stocks, had to cannibalise old casks, use the limited amount of timber imported from America or tackle the knotty problem of English oak.

One of the more ingenious solutions was the provision of pottery casks in four-and-a-half and nine-gallon sizes. The pottery body was protected by two galvanised iron rings bolted together and cushioned inside with rubber pads between the pottery and the metal to absorb shock. On the top was a screw cap. There was also increased use of much larger (108-gallon) stoneware cellar containers, which had been used by some larger pubs and clubs before the war. These were filled by pipeline from beer tankers. A few breweries also had pre-war stainless steel casks, but there was no spare metal for new ones.

Even the smallest items could present problems. The Allied Brewery Traders' Association reported early in 1941 that 'the greatest difficulty of all' had been in importing various hardwoods for making

Call for –
DRAUGHT BEER
AND HELP YOUR
COUNTRY BY SAVING –
GLASS
RUBBER
TIMBER
PETROL
LABOUR
Draught Beer is Good

TERRIFIC DRAUGHT: Brewers urged their customers to switch to draught beer from bottled. This poster was produced by Harvey's of Lewes in Sussex.

spiles (small wooden pegs) and shives (wooden bungs) for use with the casks. Softwood was also in short supply for making beer crates. Soon cases appeared constructed out of cardboard and other less robust materials. Some of these flimsy fabrications only lasted a few days. The problem was partly solved by the decline in the bottled beer market – owing to other shortages.

Bottles were in demand from every section of industry from food manufacturers to milk and medicines. The brewers came somewhere near the end of the bottling line. Bottled beer was frowned on as it was labour intensive and expensive to transport. Drinkers should make do with draught beer, was the official attitude. Rumours kept circulating that bottled beer would be withdrawn altogether. Even off-licences were encouraged to have a barrel behind the shop counter to reduce the need for bottles. The bring-a-jug brigade was back in favour.

George Birmingham, secretary of the National Federation of Off-Licence Holders' Associations, issued an open letter to the public in the summer of 1941:

If consumers showed the same consideration towards the beer

bottle as they must now perforce show towards the milk bottle, much of the difficulty would be solved. . . . Those who value their luncheon or supper appetiser will, I am sure, respond cheerfully to my appeal to them not to let the bottles bank up in the pantry, nor use them for household purposes.

The Brewers' Society responded by urging its members to increase the deposit on all bottled beer to ensure the return of the empties. There was also a movement in pubs to encourage customers to drink beer from the pump rather than the bottle. *The Brewers' Journal* even came up with the splendid slogan, 'Help the War Effort – Order Draught Beer'. This was in direct opposition to the pre-war trend in trade where bottled beer had been increasing in popularity at the expense of draught.

Alfred Leney, chairman of Fremlin's of Kent, told his AGM in Maidstone in early 1942:

Beer from the barrel is actually a better drink than from the bottle, and the cost is considerably less. For instance a pint of draught beer that can be bought for 10d would cost 1s 1d in bottle. Further, bottled beers require very much more transport. Thus you will see that labour, transport, petrol, machinery and plant would be saved by consuming draught beer in preference to bottled, and in war conditions such a course is almost a national duty.

Ansells' of Birmingham put the following advert in the Midlands Press in the summer of 1942:

From now on in all Ansell's managed houses you will only be able to obtain Ansells' in bottle on handing over an empty for every bottle you take out, and for this simple reason: bottles are scarce today and largely irreplaceable, therefore we must have them returned unless the supply of bottled beers is to fade out altogether. In your interests our managers and their staffs have strict instructions to make no exception.

But the message in a bottle does not seem to have got through to every publican, as a tale in the *Yorkshire Evening Press* in June 1943 records about one public-spirited drinker in York:

He was full of patriotic fervour and his garage floor equally full of empty beer bottles. They were relics of many a good party in recent years. One day recently he decided to take as many as he could carry in a sack to a York public house selling the same brew of beer they had originally contained. 'No, we do not want any empty bottles,' he was summarily informed, 'but so-and-so', indicating another publican, 'might accept them'.

The day was hot and the bag was heavy; even so the bottle vendor continued his errand. At the second pub he got the same reply and was advised to try a third. Here again he received a negative answer. By this time the sun was warmer, the bag heavier and the bottle carrier dismayed and disgruntled. 'Well,' he said, 'if you won't take them, may I leave them in one of your rubbish bins?' Even that request was refused. So away he went in search of a garbage heap.

The writer concluded: 'I think those bottles could have been used again. Don't you?' Perhaps the landlords were reluctant to accept the bulky bag because of the much higher deposits they now had to pay back. Charges had trebled from 1d a bottle to 3d. Much greater deposits were also placed on crates to stop them being broken up for firewood. The position had not improved by the end of the war. The *Daily Express* in April 1945, under the headline 'No beer if you don't send back the bottles', reported: 'Unless a big "Bring back your empties" drive on the part of both publicans and off-licence managers starts at once, brewers will not be able to produce even the allowed stocks of bottled beer.'

The situation was not helped, of course, by the need to supply the growing number of troops overseas with bottled beer as the war progressed. Mr M V Courage, chairman of London brewers Courage, told his AGM early in 1945:

Stockholders will, I am sure, be glad to know that we have done our best to implement the Prime Minister's promise to our fighting services, and have diverted considerable quantities of our bottled beers to supply the needs of troops overseas. I regret that this has caused a still greater shortage in the home market, which is liable to be accentuated by shortage of bottles; as you will appreciate any bottles sent overseas are not returned.

Glass was also needed for pub glasses. As early as August 1940 landlords were reporting an epidemic of thefts. 'Stolen from Tom Dancer' was the inscription one Cardiff licensee had sandblasted on his glasses in the First World War. 'We are experiencing a repetition of stealing on the same scale as then,' a publican from the Welsh capital told the *Daily Herald*. 'We may have to take drastic steps to stop the practice. Glasses are becoming so scarce that we may have to use jam jars, as we did during the last war.'

Special notices were pinned up in many bars: 'Police proceedings will immediately be taken against any person stealing glasses from these premises. Owing to war conditions glasses are very difficult to obtain, and all customers are particularly asked to exercise the utmost care to prevent breakages' They did little good.

Howard Baker, prosecuting on behalf of Mitchell's & Butler's at Birmingham police court in January 1942, revealed that during Christmas 300 glasses were stolen from one of M&B's pubs, while in another house 325 glasses were put into use one evening – and by closing time only 11 were left. This was no joke for the brewery or the licensee, particularly when half-pint glasses cost 1s and pint mugs 1s 9d. Some pubs began to charge 6d deposit and elsewhere brewers pursued the thieves to the courts. One man at Feltham in Middlesex was sent to prison for three months for taking a half-pint glass.

It was not just glass which was in short supply. Everything else related to bottled beer was scarce. The biggest bottle neck was the screw stoppers which still sealed many pint bottles. Before the war there had been one major manufacturer of these stoppers. When

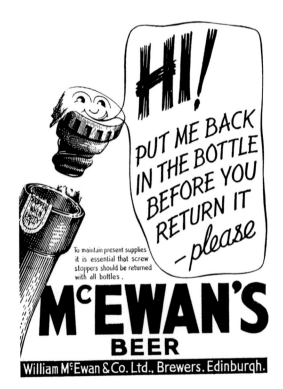

STOPPER APPEAL: McEwan's of Edinburgh used this cartoon bottle stopper to urge customers not to throw them away (*Scottish Archive*).

German planes bombed Bank Bridge Rubber Company of Manchester out of action, the Luftwaffe had hit a sensitive spot in the production line. The drinks industry was desperate. The only salvation was in the hands of the drinking public.

Bulmer's Cider placed adverts in the national press showing a screw stopper below the headline 'YOU can replace this stopper ... WE can't.' Underneath, the advert urged: 'Stoppers are made of precious rubber. A stopper lost may mean a flagon of Bulmer's less for you. Please see that empty bottles and stoppers are returned promptly to your dealer, and help us to keep up your supplies.' McEwan's of Edinburgh drew attention to the crisis through a cartoon stopper character in their adverts.

Paper was also precious. All companies economised by re-using envelopes, typing letters in single spacing and putting the carbon copy on the back of a letter under reply. Everyone collected waste paper. The Northampton Brewery Company only allowed customers into its pub concerts if they brought bundles of the stuff. *The Brewers' Journal*, with little regard to history, suggested that old brewery

WELCOME MAT:
Offiler's of Derby were the only British brewery to produce a drip mat during the war (*Geraldine David*).

ledgers and records be pulped to help the war effort.

Most advertising material like posters and showcards was dropped, though a few breweries, notably Guinness, continued to promote their products. Wood pulp beer mats, which had become popular features of pub tables in the 1930s, were discontinued. Only Offiler's of Derby produced a wartime mat with the slogan 'For wartime vitality' beneath a sketch of a soldier and a workman.

The urge to save even reached bottled beer labels. When pre-war stocks were used up many breweries introduced much smaller war-time labels. The Government believed even this was a waste, and wanted labels to be dropped altogether, arguing that the limited range of bottled beers could be identified by different coloured caps. The Ministry of Supply thought only four colours would be necessary, but after representations from the Brewers' Society this was increased to six.

Such vague markings allowed unscrupulous landlords to pass off cheaper bottled beer as a well-known brand. Guinness's brewing director John Webb later recounted one occasion when underhand tactics hit the culprit in the pocket:

At one stage during the war paper became very scarce and brewers were asked to dispense with labels on their bottles. In order to identify specific beers, coloured crown corks (metal tops) were introduced. On one occasion a representative of HM Customs and Excise asked for a Guinness at a Highgate public house. He thought it was not up to Guinness standards; so he bought two unopened bottles and brought one to the laboratory for analysis. This showed that it was not unadulterated Guinness and on our analysis he brought a prosecution against the publican.

I had to attend court to give evidence and the magistrate agreed with the evidence and fined the publican quite heavily. Just as the magistrate was giving his decision, a subdued explosion was heard and the poor publican was covered with fob from some bottles of the supposed Guinness which had exploded in his jacket pocket.

Brewers James Calder of Alloa in Scotland, on the other hand, must have wished they had followed Guinness's example and dispensed with beer labels altogether. They were prosecuted at Newcastle early in 1944 for selling beer with a cow.

Mr S Strugnell, the Chief Inspector of Northumberland, said the label on their bottled beer stated 'Milk Stout' and carried the picture of a dairy cow.

IN TROUBLE: Calder's were fined when it was discovered that their stout was not so nourishing as claimed on the label.

Even in its smaller wartime version, the label was far from modest, claiming the beer to be 'Wholesome and Invigorating.' Round the top edge was added: 'This our No.1 quality is the richest and most nourishing stout of its kind.'

'Ordinary people with no knowledge of brewing would accept the label on its face value,' said Mr Strugnell. 'There is a shortage of certain nourishing foods, and people are on the lookout for anything which may be advertised as containing nourishing ingredients.' Analysis showed the stout was ordinary stout.

Pleading guilty for the firm, Colonel A D S Rogers said that before the war ingredients for the milk stout were brought from New Zealand. Shipment was suspended by the conflict and experiments were made to find a substitute. 'Admittedly we have gone on using the labels too long and now, rather late in the day, they have been withdrawn,' he said. Calder's was fined £5 for an offence under the Food and Drugs Act.

The Scottish company must have been annoyed to have been hauled to court in the middle of a war, but there was no let-up in the law. In fact regulations proliferated during the conflict, often proving a heavy burden for smaller breweries. The system for rationing sugar was complex and constantly changing. The disposal of brewers' grains (the nutritious waste from the mash tun which provided valuable cattle feed) was almost strangled by red tape. The *Brewing Trade Review* commented on the scheme in October 1941 that 'unhappily it has become involved in the toils of the coupon rationing system with very dubious results.' A year earlier the same magazine had declared:

> Nobody enjoys filling up forms at the best of times and it is not surprising therefore that with the difficulties created by reduction in staffs, the mass of forms and returns which have had to be completed by brewers in the past year must have added to the worries of the already harassed brewers. Besides the returns on hops and barley, brewers have been required to make returns on such varied subjects as crown corks, timber and yeast.

The result of these endless forms and regulations was two-fold. Early in the war many small family breweries which had previously stayed outside the fold of the Brewers' Society joined the organisation. They felt the need of more professional advice and representation in this strange new world. Notably in 1940 and 1941 a host of Scottish companies – Murray, Usher, Jeffrey, Bernard, Drybrough, Mackay,

Robert Younger and Steel Coulson, all of Edinburgh, plus John Wright of Perth, John Fowler of Prestonpans, Gordon & Blair of Glasgow, Ballingall of Dundee, Gillespie of Dumbarton and Knox and Maclay of Alloa – were elected members.

'Those few brewers who have remained outside the Society have come to realise, as the result of war conditions, the value of the Society's organisation to the industry,' stated the Society's 1941 Annual Report. It added that those left outside included 'several hundred publican-brewers who produce beer only for their own single houses.'

By the end of the war most of these had vanished. Some had suffered from a shortage of materials or staff. But the majority had been smothered in paperwork. The piles of forms proved too intimidating to bother to continue brewing.

NO BEER TODAY
When the Glass was Empty

'This is a bad time of year to overstock,' Barclay Perkins of London warned their tenants on 31 August, 1939, 'and the brewery cannot be responsible for beers going wrong through being in stock too long.' There was little danger of that.

The clock was ticking down to the start of the Second World War and as the tension tightened some licensees began to panic. In the first days of the conflict all places of public entertainment like theatres and cinemas were closed. The pubs were packed as people drank in the dreadful news. At the same time as extra orders poured into the breweries, the Government commandeered the best brewery drays. Deliveries were a serious problem.

'Many a strange sight was witnessed in the Stag yard,' reported Watney's *Red Barrel* magazine in its notes dated 3 September, 1939. 'The brewery was besieged by every conceivable type of vehicle from motor coaches and Rolls-Royce cars to Austin Sevens and hand trucks.' Everyone was clamouring for more beer like there was no tomorrow. *The Brewers' Journal* in September 1939 reported entering one brewery. 'Emerging from the gates was a licensee in a taxicab. A cask of beer occupied the luggage space next to the driver, and the inside of the cab was filled with cases of bottled beer.'

This initial turmoil soon settled down as the black-out threw a damp, dark cloth over the excitement of war and the crowd at the bar fell away. In London, where many areas were affected by large-scale evacuation of the population, it was estimated after one year of war that beer consumption had dropped by 40 per cent.

Once the breweries had sorted out their transport difficulties, no-one was left high and dry. The fear of beer being banned or tightly rationed subsided, though the breweries had to deny persistent rumours that the Government was planning to introduce 'pool beer' (like petrol) whereby only one national brand of mild and bitter would be produced.

In December 1940, as the country faced a second war-time Christmas, *The Brewers' Journal* could confidently announce:

There will be no beer shortage, although here and there a

scarcity of bottled beer – the sales of which normally amount to gargantuan proportions at this season of the year – may be in evidence. Some brewers have cut down the different types of draught beer available in their houses in order to meet wartime difficulties but, to quote the statement issued to the press by the Brewers' Society last month, 'It is the hope and intention of every brewer to maintain his supplies of the different qualities of beer to which the public are accustomed.'

The concern was about quality not quantity. Sydney Nevile of Whitbread, the chairman of the Brewers' Society in his Annual Report that month, stressed this point in ringing terms which struck a chord with many beer drinkers:

Each of us endeavours to supply a beer of distinctive character to our customers, and to emulate our competitors in the quality of the article we produce. I attach the greatest importance to the maintenance of the individual character of our businesses, of the beers we produce, and for that reason I deprecate some of the references we have recently seen in the

TO OUR CUSTOMERS.

Owing to the greatly enlarged population, the Brewers are finding it increasingly difficult to supply sufficient beer.

We ask Customers to realize that their demands cannot always be met in full and to co-operate in order that a fair share may be enjoyed by all.

SIMPLE APOLOGY: Customers were asked to share their limited beer.

press with regard to pool beer, standard beer and such terms. I am satisfied that the public would be strongly prejudiced against the reduction of beer to one common level of pool or standard beer. Indeed, the popularity and the demand for beer would decline, and the revenue and our own businesses would suffer.

He concluded his 1940 report with the optimistic words: 'Let us hope that by the time we meet next year we shall be facing not the difficulties of war but the problems of reconstruction under peace conditions.' The problem was the war was not going to end so quickly. And as it dragged on so the shortage of supplies – and above all staff – began to bite more deeply. Within a few months the concern was all about quantity not quality. The bottomless barrel had run out.

Sir W Lindsay Everard of Everard's Brewery of Leicester announced in April 1941 that all their houses would close on Tuesdays and Thursdays. 'This decision is due to our ration of materials not being enough for an increased population,' he said. *The Brewers' Journal* reported the following month that 'Licensed houses in many Wiltshire towns are closing on one, two and even three days of the week. Some houses in Birmingham have resorted to earlier closing on certain days, whilst bottled beer is in short supply fairly generally.'

The Government was not amused. The *Daily Telegraph* reported their curt response:

The Ministry of Food has declined responsibility for whatever shortage of beer there may be in the country. It has released, it says, an agreed quantity of raw materials to the trade, and it is the business of the trade to apportion supplies to the best advantage.

The brewers blamed the sharp shifts in population. While many people had fled bombed neighbourhoods, other areas had become packed with evacuees, migrant workers and concentrations of troops, overwhelming the ability of local breweries to meet their needs. While this was true in some counties, it was far from the whole story.

The brewers had performed a miracle in maintaining supplies at the 1939 level. Despite desperate shortages of everything from bottles, barrels and cases to labour and transport, they had kept the beer lines flowing. Indeed, by reducing the strength of beer, as requested by the Government, they had increased the amount produced. The trouble was demand had gone through the brewhouse roof. Watney's *Red Barrel* magazine reported in July 1941, 'The demand for the company's draught beers has reached a level which, on several occasions recently, has proved beyond the present-day capacity of the Stag Brewery.'

One of the few benefits of war is that it obliterates unemployment. From the dark days of the Depression in the 1930s, when weary men kicked their heels on street corners, hands thrust deep into empty pockets, suddenly everyone had a job. Many were well-paid at a time when there were few consumer goods on the shelves. Despite sharp increases in the price of beer, a pint or three was within reach of almost everyone.

In those dislocated days many headed for the pub as their home from home. Once they had elbowed their way to the bar through the massed ranks of men in uniform, they found little choice. Unlike the brewers, the distillers had not been smiled on by the Government. Output was restricted to a third of the 1939 level, and most of the existing stock was earmarked for export to earn much-needed foreign currency for the country. The spirit levels behind the bar began to fall rapidly. Wine had all but vanished, imports being banned from early in the conflict.

Bonded warehouses, often in target dock areas, suffered severely in the blitz. Many cases and casks of imported wines and spirits went up in flames. Holt's Brewery of Manchester lost almost 6,000 gallons of whisky and a vast amount of port when the Manchester Bonded Warehouse in Salford was destroyed in December 1940. Five months later most of the brewery's rum was ruined when another warehouse was bombed in Liverpool. Such lost stocks of imported spirits could not be replaced until after the war.

Many commentators that long, dry summer of 1941 blamed two other phenomena for the shortage of beer. One was traditional – a sunny spell of hot, thirsty weather. The other was new – the appearance of what were termed 'pint-pot girls'. Many women were now working and discovering the delights of beer after a hard day. 'Possibly because women are earning more money and cannot spend so much on clothes, they have taken to buying drinks,' commented a brewers' spokesman. A whole new market was opening up.

The shortages themselves brought on another phenomenon – panic buying. When pubs were closed some drinkers became desperate. When the bars opened they were quickly drained to the last drop.

Draymen from the South Wales and Monmouthshire United Clubs Brewery of Pontyclun tell the not-so-tall tale of delivering a barrel to a Valleys' club which had run out of beer. By the time they had finished their complimentary glass at the bar with the steward,

SMILING THROUGH:
The beer shortage obviously
affected the *London Evening News*
cartoonist, Lee, in the summer of
1941 as he returned to the theme
time and time again.

*July 25 : "No, I don't know
where he's going, but I've
followed him for fifty miles
already."*

*July 29 : "It hasn't opened for
a week, bnt he toddles down
every night for a little wishful
drinking."*

*July 2 : "Well, he must drink
something else then. I won't have
him cluttering up the house before
half past ten."*

Another "Lee" Effort.

*Aug. 15 : " Good Evening, Mr. Bramble. Of
what will you partake to-night . . . tea or
coffee ? "*

the empty barrel was ready to take back. The thirsty miners had not waited for the cloudy beer to settle before drinking it dry.

The *London Evening News* cartoonist Lee caught the mood that parched summer with a series of cartoons showing cyclists chasing after brewers' drays, locked-out customer, and drinkers collapsing at the bar when offered tea or coffee. Equally humorous stories began to do the rounds:

A customer rushed into a pub and ordered a pint. 'Are you a regular?' asked the barmaid. To the thirsty customer's admission that he was a stranger, she replied, 'Sorry, we only serve our regulars. You might get a drink down the road.'

So down the road he went to be greeted at the next house with the question, 'Have you brought your glass?' Of course, he hadn't, so he was told: 'Well, try the White Hart by the crossroads, we only serve customers with their own glasses, we are so short.'

On he staggered to the White Hart, picked up a glass from a table, went to the bar and asked for a pint. 'Is this your glass?' said the landlord. 'Yes,' replied the exasperated customer. 'Sorry, sir, you can't have more than one pint, we're rationed now, you know.'

The brewers saw a darker side to the shortage of beer. If pubs closed their doors, they feared that the temperance movement would argue that the licences were not needed. The only Order in Council annulled during the early part of the war was the Government's proposal to open theatres and music halls on Sunday. The secretary of the Imperial Alliance for the Defence of Sunday then declared: 'Our next job is the promotion of legislation for the Sunday closing of all public houses.' A writer in the *Wine and Spirit Trade Review* recognised the peril of creeping prohibition:

I doubt whether the expedient of closing licensed premises on certain days of the week is the correct one. In recent years every effort has been made to build bigger and better public houses, with a view to providing patrons with happy and comfortable surroundings. It has been impressed upon us that the majority of those who frequent public houses do so not only for the purpose of partaking of alcoholic refreshment but because of the happy environment and cheery companionship.

If supplies are short then I suggest that the public would be better served if the supply of liquor was rationed each day, the licensee co-operating with his customers in seeing that everyone has a drink, although the quantity allowed to each customer will have to be reduced. There are those who will contend that if the public can do without alcoholic refreshment on two days a week should they not on the remaining five days a week? This seems to be the real danger.

Such warnings were largely ignored. Busy licensees, often with additional war jobs, saw no point in opening if they had no beer. In some towns new hours were agreed by the local Licensed Victuallers Associations. Leicester reduced its opening times by 18 hours a week. Glasgow decided to shut for a half-day on Thursday after 1pm. *The Scotsman* newspaper reported that 'publicans who ignored the recommendation of the trade association found early in the evening that they could not cope with the crowds, and were forced by circumstances to abandon business.'

Drinkers were far from happy. 'By whose orders and under what authority are public houses in Hull closing in the hours fixed by the local licensing bench?' thundered a correspondent to the *Hull Daily Mail*. Many were angered by back-door drinking where some pubs supplied their regulars in a back bar while keeping the public out.

Groves & Whitnall of Salford recalled in their official history published in 1949 that when beer supplies became short:

A period of almost panic drinking began. On evenings when the majority of houses in a certain area were closed, the remaining houses became packed to the doors and thousands of persons streamed into surrounding districts, searching for an open house.

In a bid to end this mad scramble, brewers, licensees and licensing justices in Manchester agreed a rationing plan. Each landlord would divide his weekly supply into nine, selling two ninths on Friday and Saturday, and one ninth on the other days of the week. This ensured that drinkers would find their local open for a while each night of the week.

Brewers' organisations wanted licensees to keep their doors open even if they had no beer. *The Brewers' Journal* praised one Midlands publican who put the following notice outside his house: 'Open to greet ye, but nowt to sell ye.' They urged landlords to try and eke out supplies. This was not always easy, as Jack Showers revealed in his book *Welcome Inn* about his popular pub near Leeds, **The Stanhope** at Rodley, which then belonged to Hey's Brewery of Bradford:

By the summer of 1941 the beer shortage was upon us and the notice 'No Beer' hung outside pubs everywhere during the week. Like most things, the scarcer it became the greater was the demand, with the result that people with cars and the petrol to spare were able to get their quota by going far and wide off the beaten track. This resulted in most places opening for only a short period, and the habit of blitz drinking soon came to affect me as well.

I rigged up two metal recorders, one on each beer dispenser, so that I could measure to the last glass my output of draught ale; by converting this into gallons and dividing the whole by seven, I was able to average my daily sales. To put this supply on sale from the moment of opening would have meant that we should have sold out in less than an hour, so I cleared my bar of all pint glasses and went on to cider and shandies. . . . The idea worked to perfection and I can honestly claim that, like the Windmill Theatre, we kept open throughout the whole of that difficult period.

The fact that we were open every night soon became known and although we had some awkward customers to deal with, who thought that they were quite within their rights to demand beer, I kept things orderly and pleasant while maintaining the legal position. Matters came to a head over the shandy question when a certain hotel made news by being fined for compelling a customer a buy a pint of shandy before he could obtain a tankard of beer; the magistrate went so far as to ask if there was a drain handy to pour the shandy down. We however kept the even tenor of our way and, that same night, in spite of banner headlines declaring 'Shandies illegal', I sold them as usual.

I well remember a certain gentleman becoming so annoyed at my refusal to give him preference that he rushed from the place, returning later with a barrister with whom he settled down and doggedly ordered beers. Of course, they were refused because the time for selling beer undiluted had not been reached. Our two hostile patrons were clearly bent on trouble so, not to be outwitted, I went to the microphone and pointed out to a packed house that I regretted having to thrust this shandy upon them but that was the only way I could remain open every night and so cater for their pleasure by retaining the show.

I further added that I ran a public house and I believed that the public were always right, after which I put to the vote the question whether they would like me to sell all my beer within a few hours, or spin it out the way I was doing. The vote was decisive. Having obtained the 'ayes' I turned upon the two miseries at the bar and called for the 'noes'. They half-ashamedly raised their hands, whereupon I took a deep breath and pointed out they were hopelessly outnumbered and were also shown up for what they were – 'just two greedy people with nothing to say.'

At this everyone roared with laughter and the two infuriated beer-hogs rushed out, like two chastened bulls, vowing frightful vengeance – namely my certain eviction within the week. Needless to say I heard nothing more.

Jack Showers kept **The Stanhope** afloat on enormous quantities of lemonade for the shandies, bulk supplies of cider and even goats' milk from his own herd. Plus a massive drop of original thinking – like dimming the lights and putting on a Punch & Judy Show to stop people going to the bar. Soon his adult customers were in second childhood. 'They were all in fits of laughter and all thought of beer was apparently for the moment forgotten.'

Home Secretary Herbert Morrison also appeared to want to forget the problem. He hoped it would go away when the hot sun set. He assured the House of Commons in July that the beer shortage was 'a transitory difficulty occasioned by increased demands due to abnormal weather conditions.' He saw no reason to expect a shortage in August or September. In fact, he was putting on a brave face. The Government was deeply concerned.

The home intelligence committee of the Ministry of Information, which monitored public morale, told the Government in a confidential report:

The beer shortage appears to be on the increase, and consternation is reported at the closing of the public houses in some towns for certain periods. In Rugby three out of four pubs are said to close one night a week. This shortage appears to have more effect upon the factory workers than any naval disaster; they interpret this shortage to mean that we are in a worse position than is being disclosed.

The chairman of Atkinson's Brewery of Birmingham, Victor Horton, later spilled the beans when he told his AGM at the end of 1941:

It is interesting to note that in districts where shortages of beer have occurred, information has been received from works managers and others that output has been adversely affected; whilst after recent enemy attacks in the Midlands we received urgent official requests to send more beer to the particular districts.

The brewing industry was certainly not remotely convinced by assurances that the shortages would soon disappear. They knew the facts. *The Brewers' Journal* reported in August 1941:

The beer shortage problem, in many areas at any rate, is likely to prove chronic rather than acute . . . as time proceeds it is inevitable that beer will be left more and more to fill the bill (due to the embargo on imported wines and spirits). Licensees today get only 50 per cent of their 1940 purchases of whisky and are fortunate if they secure two-thirds of their 1940 gin supplies. British wines are in short supply; brandies are almost unprocurable. As to ports and sherries, 30 per cent of 1940 supplies perhaps represents the allocation of the average licensee. Even so, as some of these supplies are withdrawals from stock, the only safe forecast is that less rather than more of the favourite rivals to the national beverage will be available as time proceeds. Today even minerals and other soft drinks are scarce. The winter will see cider dearer and relatively in short supply.

The *Journal* also believed the beer shortage was here to stay because of other more fundamental factors:

Today unemployment has faded into relative insignificance. Wages have bounded to new high levels; probably more wage earners are on the pay rolls than ever before. Normally the steep increase in the price of beer – brought about by the raising of the beer duty thrice since September 1939 – would have served to peg demand to the available beer supplies. But a new factor has entered into the situation, namely the rationing of food and clothing combined with the limitation placed upon virtually all classes of goods.

The working classes probably have a fuller purse today than at any time since the last war. Women too are employed in numbers hitherto unparalleled and are moreover engaged in more arduous work than ever before . . . in increasing numbers they have joined the ranks of those who appreciate the value attaching to an evening glass of beer. Indeed, with regard to the populace in general, they have not been slow to realise that beer adds a welcome relish to a diet made far more monotonous by war-time conditions.

Small wonder then that in all these circumstances today's beer output, limited as it is . . . is proving inadequate to meet present-day demands.

The situation could only get worse as another factor came increasingly into play. The need to supply a growing number of troops, both at home and overseas. Demand continued to soar, with different parts of the country competing for the title of the driest spot in Britain.

Lord Woolton's reaffirmation in September 1942 that there would be no beer rationing was irrelevant. The simple fact was there was not enough ale to go round. That month in Nottingham, miners' representatives told licensing magistrates that output was being held up because miners were fed up with finding pubs shut. A policeman confirmed their story. 'There seems to be less beer in Nottingham than anywhere else: public houses open three days a week, and when open are besieged.'

As the war ground on many breweries ceased to press their licensees to stay open. Captain C E H Master, chairman of Friary, Holroyd & Healy's Breweries of Guildford in Surrey, declared in September 1944:

It has been suggested by some licensing benches that houses should remain open for the full permitted hours, but when as is often the case, they have been drained dry by the sudden incursion of thirsty troops, and in consequence have no beer, no spirits, no cigarettes, no food for sale nor minerals, it would seem rather a waste of light, heat and services to keep them open, especially as the public often become incensed if they find houses open with nothing to sell.

Yet the fermenting vessels were full to creaking. By 1944 production was running at record levels for the war. In the three months to 30 June over eight million bulk barrels were rolled out – a third of the amount produced in the whole of 1939. Yet still the breweries could not keep up with demand. 'The published figures create an exasperating mirage and tongues will protrude to new and record levels,' commented *The Economist* magazine. 'Only Tantalus has suffered in comparable degree.'

The shortage had not gone away. It had got worse. 'During the past two months the news value of beer has risen to unprecedented

VICTORY BREWS: Only five breweries produced special bottled beers to mark the end of the war in 1945 – Barclay's of London; Greenall Whitley of Warrington; Ruddle's of Rutland; John Smith's of Tadcaster and the Wrexham Lager Beer Company. The rest were too exhausted. Or had no bottles.

heights. The daily and Sunday newspapers, the weekly and periodical press, have fanned the subject into a flame of interest,' said *The Brewers' Journal* in September 1944. 'The press hubbub has been occasioned by a beer shortage more acute than any experienced during the present war.'

With victory in sight, rumours circulated that pubs would not even open on Armistice Day. The breweries strongly denied this. *The Brewers' Journal* proclaimed:

It would be unthinkable that this centre of social life, where men and women foregathered in the dark days of the war for mutual courage and encouragement, and to arm themselves for the trials of tomorrow, should close its doors on the day of liberation from the direst peril that ever has beset this land.

But few breweries sought any extension to celebrate the victory. They knew they would be hard pressed to supply enough beer during normal opening hours.

In the event, VE Day and the following day's holiday were celebrated in style. A few breweries like Barclay's of Southwark even brought out a special victory beer to mark the occasion. But most breweries also closed down, exhausted, for the two-day holiday, and the celebrations ushered in 'a beer shortage quite unparalleled during the war' in London, which was packed with returning troops and evacuees. Many pubs in the capital were only able to trade four days out of seven after the holiday, noted *The Brewers' Journal* in August 1945.

The war might have ended in Europe, but the 'No Beer' notices remained firmly fixed in the bar windows.

BETTER THAN BULLETS
Beer to the Troops

The inspecting officer looked long and hard down the line of men, before turning to the sergeant:

'What precautions do you take against infected water, sergeant?'

Sergeant: 'First, we boil it, sir.'

Officer: 'Good.'

Sergeant: 'Then we filter it.'

Officer: 'Excellent.'

Sergeant: 'And then, sir, we drink beer.'

One part of the war effort was never going to accept 'No Beer' notices – the soldiers at the sharp end of the military machine. Prime Minister Winston Churchill fully understood their feelings.

In a note to the Secretary of State for War in November 1944, following thirsty complaints from Italy, he thundered: 'Make sure that the beer – four pints a week – goes to the troops under fire before any of the parties in the rear get a drop.' Beer was almost as important as bullets, it seemed, when it came to defeating the enemy.

This had even been understood in the First World War. When tight restrictions were imposed on the amount of beer brewers could produce, these rules did not apply to ale for military canteens. When in the last year of the war in 1918, the average gravity of beer was reduced to the weak figure of 1030, army and navy bars were again exempt. The average gravity of their beer was fixed at the much stronger rate of 1045. Soldiers and sailors, it was felt, deserved a more sustaining drop than the folk back home.

At the beginning of the Second World War, when the British Expeditionary Force sat secure in its complacency behind the French Maginot Line, there was no difficulty in supplying the troops. The British Tommy could enjoy French beer. 'Although he can have white and red wines of excellent quality for less money than beer, he calls with gusto for his "bock" or "demi", words that the lads have learned with speed,' reported *The Brewers' Journal* in October 1939.

The French brewers distributed leaflets to the British troops, attempting to explain their products. 'French beer is well known for its great lightness. It contains a perfect proportion of alcohol, sugar, peptones and carbonic gases. . . . The diuretic qualities of French beer eliminate uric acid and assure a greater freeness of the joints.'

Perhaps alarmed by these supple claims, some soldiers complained that the French blonde beers were not like the nut brown ale of home, and arrangements were made to brew British-style beers in French breweries. Meanwhile crates of bottled beer were exported from Britain. Everyone relaxed with a glass and waited for the Germans to surrender. Chamberlain believed he could blockade Hitler into submission.

The 'Phoney War' was no less intense in the House of Commons. Colonel Evans, the Conservative MP for Cardiff South, was concerned that the troops across The Channel were being overcharged for exported British beer. When the men first arrived in France the price was 8½d a pint. By March 1940 it was down to 5d. As war raged in the East, a famous victory had been won against the NAAFI in the West.

Mr Macquisten, the Conservative MP for Argyll, believed the cost could drop even further to a penny a pint if the beer was brewed by the army itself behind the lines 'as farmers brewed it in England.' Sir Victor Warrender, the Financial Secretary to the War Office, asked Mr Macquisten to send details of this remarkable scheme. 'May we add that every brewer in England would be grateful to receive the recipe for performing this miracle,' added The Brewers' Journal.

The temperance movement, annoyed by all this talk about booze for the troops, declared that drink might prove a threat to security by loosening the tongues of unwary privates. This did not worry senior officers. 'The British soldier can always be trusted to take his glass of beer without any risk of giving away the small amount of knowledge about the war in his possession,' said Major-General Sir John Kennedy in the Weekly Scotsman in February 1940. If only the army commanders had possessed a greater knowledge of modern warfare.

When the German Panzers in May 1940 sliced through the Allies' defences like a knife through the frothy head on a glass of French beer, the harsh reality of war hit home. The British Expeditionary Force was cut off and scrambled home from Dunkirk, leaving most of its equipment behind. Brewers in Northern France were left with hundreds of barrels of British-style beer just as German troops roared past on their way to Paris.

The small number of British breweries which specialised in the export trade had been doing bumper business early in 1940, thanks to the troops in France and the fact that one of their main rivals, Germany, had been cut off from the world market. Then two other significant players – Denmark and The Netherlands – had been knocked out of contention when they were invaded. The Board of Trade was eager to see more exports to the United States. Labels carrying the Union Jack and the slogan 'Britain Delivers the Goods' were stuck on cases of Scotch whisky.

'We should like to see a drive made to introduce into the United States under this slogan certain specialised brands of high-gravity beers,' commented *The Brewers' Journal* in December 1940. The magazine believed they 'might enjoy a vogue there at a time when things British are looked upon with particular favour.' The Government initially promised to provide extra brewing materials, cans and cases for this business – but then changed its mind, introducing restrictions and eventually prohibiting the export of beer. In part this was because of shortages at home, but mostly because of the need to direct export supplies to British troops fighting abroad and to those forces building up inside Britain, now including growing numbers of American soldiers.

A 'Beer for Troops' Committee was set up in July 1942 by the Brewers' Society at the request of the Ministry of Food. The chairman was Mr F A Simonds of the Reading brewers, Simonds, a company

THIRST OBJECTIVE: Troops were always after beer at home as this 1943 Bateman cartoon demonstrates. Pubs could quickly run dry.

experienced both in supplying military canteens and in the export trade. At first its main concern was to quench the thirsts of the troops massing at home.

'It is a national duty that every brewer should do his utmost to supply beer for troops in their messes, many of which are a long distance from the nearest licensed premises,' urged the Brewers' Society's Annual Report for 1942. 'To a large extent these supplies are arranged locally, but the Society has undertaken to make the best arrangements possible to find supplies where these cannot be provided by brewers in the neighbourhood.'

Supplying NAAFI canteens at home was awkward at a time of beer shortages; supplying beer to troops beyond these islands was another problem altogether. No longer were they just across The Channel. The battlefronts had moved to much more distant lands on other continents like Asia and Africa.

In January 1941 British forces advanced along the North African coast from Egypt, seizing Tobruk in Libya and defeating a much larger Italian army. It was the first welcome taste of victory on the ground for the bombed and battered people back home. Perhaps the war was turning.

The Allied advance, stiffened by a strong contingent of Australian troops, reached as far as Benghazi. There, according to *The Brewers' Journal*, a welcome surprise awaited them. 'Beer may soon be on sale to British and Imperial forces in Libya, as in Benghazi our troops found a brewery in good working order. NAAFI is now negotiating for the entire output of the brewery,' reported the magazine in March 1941.

They had little time to drink to their success. The Germans entered North Africa and pushed the British back to the walls of Tobruk. There they dug in, determined not to lose their last remaining gain. The port was cut off by land and besieged by Rommel. Yet Tobruk held out for months and became a name to conjure with, like Mafeking in the Boer War. It was claimed to be the longest siege in British history, lasting eight months. A name to lift morale.

In October 1941 two London breweries – Whitbread and Watney – determined to recognise this heroic resistance. They sent 35 tons of bottled beer as a gift in the hope that it would arrive by Christmas. Each of the bottles in the 500 cases was specially marked 'Best wishes to the Defenders of Tobruk.' The beer got through and was warmly welcomed.

Mr Spink of the South Notts. Hussars, who had been out fighting in the Middle East for over two years, wrote:

LOAD OF CHEER: Workers toast the lorry-load of Watney and Whitbread beer sent to Tobruk (*Courage Archive*).

It was sure a treat to taste once more real English beer. It is much better than the Egyptian stuff we get out here, and won't we be glad when we can drink regularly in the country where it is brewed. We thought it was a fine gesture to send us the beer and we all thank them many times.

WELCOME DROP: A label from one of the bottles of beer sent to the troops in Tobruk (*Whitbread Archive*).

The gesture was remembered for many years. In 1982 Mr G F Putley wrote to Whitbread:

On November 11, 1941, whilst serving with the 1st Battalion The Essex Regiment in Tobruk, every man was issued with a bottle of Double Brown Ale with the compliments of Whitbread & Co. This has never been forgotten by me for two reasons. Firstly, November 11 happens to be our wedding anniversary, and I was able to have a drink on that particular day. Secondly, I have kept the label from the bottle for 41 years to the day. I managed to carry the label throughout the remainder of my foreign service, even as a Chindit in the Burma Campaign.

Another soldier from The Essex Regiment commented: 'It was quite a treat and well appreciated, I can assure you, by all. Boosted our morale quite a lot. . . .'

The reaction underscored what the military authorities already knew – supplies of beer were vital for the British troops, particularly in hot countries. By the end of 1941 shipments were being prepared for forces not only in Libya and Egypt, but also in Iraq and Iran. 'These shipments are being made on order of the British Government as a result of the discovery made by Lord Allenby during the last war that beer was an essential part of the rations of the soldiers under his command,' reported *The Brewers' Journal* in December 1941.

Some of the beer came from American and Canadian breweries which had more bottling and canning capacity. The Americans painted their cans dull green, known as 'olive drab', in order not to attract the attention of the enemy. Felinfoel Brewery of Llanelli, which had pioneered beer canning in Europe in 1935, also entered the Mediterranean theatre of war. One of the few cargoes to break the German siege of Malta contained welcome cans of their Welsh ale for the parched Llanelli Territorials manning the anti-aircraft guns.

Relatively few other British breweries had established canning lines before the war, but those who had were in great demand, particularly from the Merchant and Royal Navy as canned beer was lighter and took up less space than bottled beer in the cramped ships. By the end of 1945 Barclay's Brewery of Southwark had supplied nearly 40 million cans to the naval forces.

On dry land, the NAAFI created a chain of strange road houses along the dusty highway in North Africa, which must have had more than one soldier rubbing his eyes in the belief he was seeing a mirage. 'Spaced at intervals of many miles along the sandy desert roads, the houses are being made to resemble English public houses, two of them being called **Noah's Ark** and **The Man in the Moon**,' reported *The Brewers' Journal*. 'To meet the shortage of drinking glasses, surplus beer bottles have been cut down to pint size, with milled edges.'

In deeper, darker corners of Africa there were no such luxuries as mock English pubs – or even beer as Europeans knew it. *The Brewers' Journal* reported in January 1943 that Allied troops 'are probably enjoying some odd experiences in the matter of potable ale.' This was Kaffir beer 'which is called variously chonala, pombe and walwa and is not, in fact, a bad substitute for the genuine article once the taste for it has been acquired.' This millet-based brew deserved respect, warned the magazine:

It is on record that a well-known traveller experimented with a potful of the undiluted liquor and was reduced to a staggering condition. Today it is usually diluted and whilst a shilling buys a large calabash full, for a florin enough is bought to prostrate the entire camp for a week.

By July 1942, at the time the Beer for Troops Committee was established in Britain to co-ordinate supplies, the NAAFI was obtaining beer from some 200 British breweries, most for military canteens in the United Kingdom. The main problems were obtaining enough beer and sufficient transport as many of the camps were in remote areas and, under official rules, war department vehicles were not allowed to deliver the barrels.

The supply system worked on a purely voluntary basis. The Brewers' Society Council paid tribute to this in their Annual Report for 1943:

The council fully realise that most breweries find it difficult to keep their own houses supplied, and that it is only at some sacrifice of their own customers that they can meet these demands for beer for the troops. Nevertheless, the council has strongly urged that all brewers should do their utmost to help when called upon.

This voluntary approach was in sharp contrast to America where the United States Food Distribution Administration (FDA) had ordered the brewing industry to set aside 15 per cent of all beer brewed for the armed forces. This large amount meant that the GI received more beer than the civilian. The FDA also stipulated that the gravity should be around 1045, considerably stronger than British wartime brews. British breweries which produced beer for the growing number of US units in Britain received special supplies of American malt and hops.

It was by now widely accepted that beer was best for the troops. But this did not mean that there were no outbreaks of outrage from time to time. When in November 1943 repatriated prisoners of war were given bottles of beer by the Red Cross after their arrival at Liverpool and Leith, some teetotallers protested that this was a misuse of the organisation's funds. The charity's secretary replied:

The object of the Red Cross was to give the returning prisoners a thoroughly British meal for those who were well enough to partake of it. Tea and coffee and other beverages were provided for all who wanted them. The fact that the BBC announced that 4,000 bottles of beer had been provided made people think that much more had been supplied than was necessary to give each man one pint. This was not so. In fact there was not enough for all who returned to have one pint each.

The Red Cross's concluding comments demonstrated how far the temperance movement had been sidelined:

We do not for a moment question the genuineness of the feelings of those who protest, but such protests come from a section of the community definitely committed to a line of policy based on their own particular opinions and cannot be taken as in any way reflecting the opinion of the community as a whole.

The House of Commons rang with protests of a different kind. Sir Leonard Lyle asked the Secretary of State for War on 30 November, 1943: 'Is the right honourable gentleman aware that a considerable time after the Salerno landing [in Italy] there was only one bottle for every four men? Is he not aware that beer is very necessary for troops undergoing such conditions?' The next day Sir Archibald Knox asked the Secretary of State for Air 'whether he is aware that airmen in North Africa complain that they can only get one pint of English beer a week to drink?' He added: 'I have had a letter from the commander of a squadron who says that morale is likely to suffer if these troops do not get beer.' Both ministers replied that they were doing all they could to increase supplies.

In June 1944, as the nation waited in hope and fear for the invasion of Europe, the *Brewing Trade Review* listed all the problems facing the industry and then concluded:

But we do believe that a further last ounce of effort could produce a valuable degree of help. Large numbers of our men and those of our Allies are awaiting the order to attack. As they go forward and others step up into their places, they deserve the best that the industry can do for them. We believe that we can rely on the industry and on brewery employees to put forward that last ounce.

That last ounce of effort weighed in with some ingenious methods of delivering beer – and some generous gestures.

When the troops hit the Normandy beaches on 6 June, 1944, the beer was not far behind. Indeed, a number of barrels were flown in on D-Day, hung below the wings of fighter planes.

Bushell, Watkins & Smith of Westerham in Kent proudly kept a barrel on display at the brewery for many years beneath a plaque

BARRELS AWAY: A fighter plane takes off for the front across The Channel with casks of beer hanging below (*Whitbread Archive*).

STRONG STUFF: A close-up of a cask of beer from Strongs' of Romsey fixed beneath the wing (*Whitbread Archive*).

```
        A  GIFT
  TO  OUR  FIGHTING  FORCES
            FROM
  MITCHELLS & BUTLERS LIMITED,
         BIRMINGHAM.
  _____
  BEST   OF   LUCK
  _____
  IF THIS CASK IS RETURNED WE WILL REFILL
  AND SEND BACK TO YOU.   REPLACE CORK.
```

TEMPTING PROMISE:
Mitchell's & Butler's sent this card with each cask delivered to Normandy, with the pledge that if returned the cask would be refilled and sent back (*Bass Museum*).

declaring, 'This cask containing Westerham Bitter was flown to France, D-Day, June 6, 1944, by the Royal Air Force.' Bushell's regularly supplied the mess at Biggin Hill from where some of the planes flew on the fatal day. What surprised the brewery was that the empty cask was returned from the new battle front.

Other breweries along the South Coast were involved in this vital drop to the front-line, including The Star Brewery of Eastbourne, Henty & Constable of Chichester in Sussex and Strongs' of Romsey in Hampshire.

Much of this ferrying by fighter pilots was unofficial. In order to fool paper pushers in the offices some pilots called the cask cargo hanging from the bomb racks 'XXX Depth Charge'. As the barrels were easily spotted from the ground some Spitfires instead carried beer in their spare long-range fuel tanks – but not everyone enjoyed their pint with a pronounced petrol aroma.

On a more official basis, Mitchell's & Butler's Cape Hill Brewery sent 2,000 casks to Normandy from Birmingham as a generous gift to the front-line troops. Each carried a card with the tempting promise: 'If this cask is returned, we will refill and send back to you.'

Meanwhile the NAAFI and the brewing industry worked overtime to get bottled beer through to the troops. In order to conserve supplies a complete ban had been placed on all commercial exports in May 1944. Packing stations were established, notably in London in premises donated by Simonds of Reading. Companies familiar with the export trade had pasteurising equipment to ensure their bottled beers could withstand long journeys and delays in transport. Most British breweries were not geared up for this business.

Brandon's Putney Brewery (part of Mann's of London) replied in July 1944 to the Brewers' Society's request for beer for NAAFI

CRATE EFFORT: Women at work at the London packing station for 'Beer for the Troops' inside Simonds' London depot in 1944. The half-pint bottles were packed 32 to a box in four layers of eight bottles between moulded paper sheets cushioned by wood chips.

overseas, 'We have no pasteurising plant on these premises.' The brewery was struggling to cope with its own local demand. 'In any event the quantity of 67 barrels per week would not apply under present conditions owing to the numerous stoppages of work through the revival of enemy action (flying bombs).'

Many breweries were completely exhausted by the war. So were their beers. Their weak strength meant they did not survive for long. Charles Beasley's North Kent Brewery of Plumstead replied to the same circular:

> While we shall be only too pleased to supply our share of half-pint bottled beer for NAAFI overseas, we cannot guarantee that our bottled beers at their present gravities will remain in condition for more than three weeks. Our pasteuriser, which was installed in 1930, and is much worn, has been working right up to capacity for the past five years, supplying beers in the munition areas of Erith, Woolwich, Dartford and Crayford, leaving no time for overhaul other than minor repairs.

Such problems meant the main burden of supplying the troops fell on the traditional exporting breweries (like Hope & Anchor of Sheffield and Guinness) plus the main London breweries which boasted large-scale pasteurising plants. Their domestic bottled beer trade was diverted to the NAAFI and by October 1944 the London packaging station had already sent out 11,000 cases. Mitchell's & Butler's of Birmingham also chipped in with extensive supplies, their 'Marvellous Beer' being enjoyed from Tromso in the Arctic Circle to the jungles of Borneo. By 1945 the Cape Hill Brewery estimated it had sent some 3,250,000 bottles abroad.

The effort was much appreciated. A staff officer wrote from Normandy in August 1944:

> Yesterday was a scorcher, and it was really delightful to see the pleasure in the faces of all ranks when it was found that bottled beer was on sale for the first time. I am told by friends from many quarters that it has been welcome all along the front, and has done more to raise the morale of the troops than the issue of bread. The troops have had some very tough fighting and deserve the best we can give them.

As the Continental campaigns developed, the demand for beer for the troops grew larger and larger. In November 1944 the Government ordered that supplies must be increased to about five per cent of all home production, with all beer with a shelf life of more than six weeks to be made available to the NAAFI.

Guinness lent their trade manager Will Phillips to the Brewers' Society to organise the massive operation. His formidable job was to widen the burden by getting more breweries involved. All were expected to provide some beer, even if this meant leaving their home trade short. The troops came first. He also had to sort out chronic shortages of bottles, cases and labour. He co-opted another Guinness employee James Milner who recalled their tricky task:

There was at the time a lot of ill-informed comment and many people were angered by the sight of a delivery of beer to a pub, instead of being sent to the troops, as they did not realise that beer brewed for quick consumption at home would be acid and undrinkable by the time it reached a destination abroad.

Four official packing stations were established at Whitbread in London, Mitchell's & Butler's in Birmingham, Hope & Anchor in Sheffield ('the most efficient one,' claimed Mr Milner) and William Younger's in Edinburgh. Beer needed to remain sound for three months for Europe and nine months for the Far East. It was a vast operation. One single shipment from Whitbread filled 47 railway trucks with 268,000 bottles. There were many awkward problems. Lack of communication in the chaos of war was one, as Mr Milner recalled:

Younger's of Edinburgh used to ship their pale ale to India in casks, and when empty the casks were broken down to save shipping space and returned to the brewery. They told me that if they could get one of their coopers out of the army (to reconstruct the casks), they could increase supplies to the NAAFI. So I asked the Ministry of Food to apply for this man's release. After a while, word came that this man could not be released, so I rang Mr Bruce of Younger's. He replied to my

JOINING UP: Hope and Anchor Breweries of Sheffield became the northern packaging station for 'Beer for the Troops'. Its own Jubilee Stout followed the forces wherever they went; 1,000 gallons a week being exported after D-Day.

astonishment that the man had been working at the brewery for the past two weeks and he hoped that the army were getting the same good value from his services that they were!

As the Western front widened, it became increasingly difficult to meet the demands of the growing numbers of troops with bottled beer from Britain. The supply of bottles became acute, as few were returned from the front and the British glass industry could not make enough to meet war-time demand.

Increasingly reliance was placed on another policy. British breweries instead were required to provide stocks of malt and hops for use in liberated breweries in France, Italy and Belgium. 'This course represents a considerable saving in transport as compared with the shipment of beer, and as production from the local breweries can be developed it will ease the demand for beer from this country,' commented *The Brewers' Journal* in December 1944. Some British brewing staff were sent out to help get production underway on plant long closed by the war.

As more breweries opened on the Continent in 1945 the main problem area became the much longer supply lines to the Far East, where the war against Japan threatened to rage much longer than in Europe.

This hot and sticky arena demanded more ingenious solutions.

DAVY JONES' DELIGHT
The Floating Brewery

The fighting forces in the Far East often felt themselves to be the forgotten army of the Second World War. Battling away in the jungle half a world from home, they were not only at the end of the supply line but at the bottom of most priority lists.

When Singapore was captured by the Japanese in February 1942, its fall reflected years of neglect. The sun was setting on the British Empire as fast as the morale of the troops was dipping below the horizon. And there was little to lift spirits and refresh parched throats.

The Far East needed top-quality beer which could last for 9 to 12 months; it had to be capable of surviving high temperatures, rough handling and long voyages. In 1938 Britain had exported 200,000 barrels of beer in bottle. This modest amount was never going to be enough for wartime demands, and with the European conflict taking the lion's share of supplies, the more distant troops were often left to lick their cracked lips.

The situation was not helped by the lack of local breweries. Unlike in Europe these were few and far between. India had attempted to introduce prohibition just before the Second World War and the political leaders were hostile to British rule, demanding independence. Co-operation was in short supply.

Lieutenant Clarkson, who had been outside manager for the Openshaw Brewery of Manchester before the war, recalled the changing and constricting market in India. When he arrived in 1941, British beer was still widely available, notably Allsopp's from Burton, Barclay's from London and McEwan's and Tennent's from Scotland. As these ran out they were replaced by local Indian brands – and for a while even by beer from Japan.

By the end of 1942 rationing was introduced, each man receiving just three bottles a month. This restriction was keenly felt. Lieutenant Clarkson reported:

> The beer issue is naturally a matter of paramount importance to the troops who are fighting in temperatures never below 80 degrees and up to 120 degrees in the sun, and in areas where the water has to be carried up in tanks and water boats.

By the end of 1944 local Indian production had been expanded by 300 per cent, with the bulk of the beer directed to the armed forces. The Murree Brewery of Rawalpindi, for instance, had, over five years, supplied more than 1,680,000 dozen quarts 'which is indeed creditable when one realises how small our plant originally was,' claimed the company.

But the Earl of Munster, in a report dealing with amenities for troops in the Far East published in December 1944, declared that this was still not enough even to provide each man with his meagre three bottles a month. This was partly because of a shortage of brewing materials and other supplies at the local breweries. The Murree Brewery was temporarily forced to close down in February 1945 as it had run out of coal, so depriving the armed forces of 1,500 dozen bottled beers a day, not to mention draught beer for the local area. Substantial imports from other countries were the only answer, decided Lord Munster.

This conclusion annoyed the hard-pressed local breweries, who were also angered by disparaging remarks made about the quality of Indian beer. The Murree Brewery wrote to the Minister of Food, Colonel Llewellin, in protest:

The beer manufactured by this company compares more than favourably with any imported beer from England or elsewhere, and this justifiable claim may be substantiated by reference to the officers and men who were lucky enough to obtain Murree beer in their allotment. . . . It is high time that justice was given to those who have really produced an article worthy of the best brewery traditions. . . . It is 100 per cent malt and of an alcoholic content considerably higher by far than that of beers at present brewed in England. This type of beer has proved eminently satisfactory for export and for the hard, trying conditions beer is exposed to in a country like India.

Had an adequate supply of essential materials for the manufacture of beer and necessary assistance been afforded us, the production of beer as far as this company is concerned, would have been greatly enhanced.

The prices reflected beer's rarity. By the summer of 1945, when Australian and American brands had largely taken over, a bottle cost 1s 3d a pint or more. 'Only last Sunday I was charged 5s 3d for a quart of Australian beer,' Lieutenant Clarkson wrote from Bombay in June 1945.

'The result of the acute shortage of beer and spirits has produced the usual local brands of so-called spirits,' he added. 'Most of these are on a par with American Prohibition products and anybody drinking them does so at his own risk – fortunately the authorities have warned the troops against drinking them.'

The military tried to produce their own home-brew for troops in the jungle frontline. Lord Louis Mountbatten introduced mobile breweries for his forward forces in Burma. The equipment was fixed on the back of 15-hundredweight trucks and included a scaled-down boiler, mash tun, copper, cooler and fermenting vessels. 'Three days are taken in the process and the beer keeps only for 12 hours, but the results are said to be good notwithstanding a temperature of 95 degrees in the shade,' reported the *Brewing Trade Review* in January 1944.

This ingenious attempt to supply combat units with a 'beery beverage' was still in the experimental stage a year later. 'A form of portable brewery has been evolved in which a type of beer acceptable to the troops can be brewed,' reported *The Brewers' Journal* in January 1945. 'Two sets of this equipment are undergoing tests in field service conditions. Further equipment can be made available if the experiments prove satisfactory.'

The army even attempted to take the atmosphere of the traditional English pub to the frontline through a film entitled 'Down at the George'. Filming began at a home-brew pub, the **Moor Park Hotel** in Garstang Road, Preston, in January 1945. Landlord Henry Wilson's house was chosen because of its 'homely atmosphere', said the War Office.

Another attempt to make up for the shortage of beer was the development of potent substitutes, notably the production of 'Cydrale' from fermented fruit. The Indian breweries were disgusted by such experiments. The general manager of the Murree Brewery, Mr A Ebeling, commented:

> As a technical brewer of 26 years standing of which some 22 years have been spent in India, the proposal (for portable breweries) is really too amusing to bear comment. If our beer manufactured under the most scientific conditions is considered poor, what can be expected from these portable breweries?

But such experiments were necessary, as it was proving impossible to get enough beer through to the scattered forward forces, either from imports or local Indian breweries, which were increasingly being left far behind the fighting. The Murree Brewery was in the distant north-west of India close to the border with Afghanistan, in an area which was later to become Pakistan.

The Earl of Munster on his return from India told the House of Lords on 18 April, 1945:

The question of a sufficient provision of beer is one of the greatest difficulty. Enormous efforts have been made to increase exports to India and South-East Asia Command and the quantity given to these commands has greatly increased. Nevertheless, it is not yet up to the target figure which has been laid down. Noble Lords who know India are well aware of the difficulty of distributing immense quantities of goods. With the very long lines of communication over which we are now operating, it is inevitable that there must be some local disparities in the supply of beer, but we are doing everything possible to overcome these difficulties.

One idea being floated was floating breweries. If the brewhouses in Britain and India were left too far behind, why not sail a brewery into the combat zone to provide rest and recreation for the tired troops? Remarkably, this surprising scheme was hammered into reality against tremendous odds. Even if, in the end, it sailed to the rescue a little late.

In part, its success was due to Hitler's air raids on Britain. When the Luftwaffe had bombed Southampton, the fermenting room of Cooper's East Street Brewery had been completely destroyed. In order to maintain production, brewer Stephen Clarke devised a special 'pressure fermentation' system in enclosed conditioning tanks. This experimental system needed less vessels and was adopted for the confined shipboard brewery, the fermentation chambers doubling as carbonating and conditioning tanks.

The plans for brewing at sea had been launched in 1944 by the Royal Navy. They had pushed the brewing boat out on their own, instructing brewery engineers Adlams of Bristol to design a suitable plant using malt extract capable of brewing 250 barrels a week.

A supply of suitable water was not a problem as the navy had already mastered the art during the previous war years of changing sea water into fresh water by distillation. Five tons of fresh water could be produced through the use of one ton of fuel oil.

Experimental brews were carried out by Mr Clarke in Southampton and by Bernard Dixon of Green's Brewery in Luton. The Admiralty were thinking big, having ordered four plants with the possibility of a further six. A flotilla of floating breweries was fermenting in the minds of the Sea Lords.

The bold scheme was born out of desperation, owing to the acute shortage of suitable beer. The NAAFI needed 23,200 barrels a month of export quality bottled beer for the Far East, but only 13,000 were being supplied and there was little hope of making good the shortfall of 10,000 barrels in the immediate future. Beer of this quality needed to mature for at least three months, and new plant would be required to expand production in Britain. The NAAFI was also reluctant to accept stout as part of the normal allocation for troops, even though the dark beer accounted for 10 per cent of the available export supplies.

The Royal Navy was planning for a long war. While Hitler was being forced back into his final bunker in Berlin as the Allied forces advanced from the West and the Soviet army rolled in from the East, the Japanese were still formidable foes. The war in the Far East was expected to last at least 18 months after Germany had surrendered in Europe.

Much to its annoyance, the Brewers' Society was only consulted about the floating breweries scheme late in 1944 when the Admiralty needed qualified brewers to run the planned plants. The society's chairman, Colonel C J Newbold of Guinness, arranged for Lance McMullen, who had been a pre-war brewer at St James's Gate in Dublin, to act as liaison officer from January 1945, working for the Admiralty's director of victualling. He was to supervise the construction of the plant at Adlams in Bristol.

Colonel Newbold also arranged for the brewing materials to be tested at Guinness's Park Royal Brewery in London, using their extensive laboratory and miniature brewery. It was just as well. To save space the equipment had been designed without a mash tun. The shipboard brewery would use ready-prepared malt extract and hop concentrate. It could have been a sticky experience without Guinness's trial brews, as technical director Dr John Webb recalled after they had tested various malt extracts: 'This we did, making a quite acceptable drink, with the exception of the produce of one manufacturer whose malt extract contained an infection.' This caused the extract to ferment inside its sealed containers, 'producing a lot of carbon dioxide, which made the tins in which it was delivered quite explosive.' The last thing wanted on board ship were exploding drums of treacle.

More worryingly, the plant had been designed without any provision for maintaining a sound supply of yeast, vital for brewing beer. Lance McMullen reported after his first visit to Bristol:

Whereas the brewery as a whole seemed sound enough, there appeared to be a serious omission in that no arrangements had been made for producing enough yeast to start brewing with on board nor, assuming that it had been started with yeast from an outside source (Guinness later supplied the yeast) was there any way of keeping the yeast going if for any reason there should be an interruption of more than about nine days between full-sized brews.

This flaw, which could have scuppered the whole project if it had not been detected at an early stage, was tackled by the provision of laboratory equipment by Guinness – and by building a miniature (100-gallon) brewery on the same lines as the main plant to keep the yeast going when the ship's brewery was not in operation.

As the problems mounted, the Sea Lords began to get wet feet. The anxious Admiralty wanted the Brewers' Society or a commercial brewery to take responsibility for the project. But no company was willing to lend its name to an experimental scheme and guarantee the quality of beer brewed under testing conditions on the other side of the world.

The original ambitious plans were whittled down to two floating breweries and one shore-based plant, with the NAAFI reluctantly agreeing to take control.

The Brewers' Society were asked to send a committee of experts to Bristol to review the plans. Walter Scott, the managing director of Ansell's Brewery of Birmingham, along with the head brewer of London brewers Charrington, Mr AC Reavenall, duly visited Adlams early in March 1945.

Walter Scott was not impressed when he saw the sketches. He felt the plant was too complicated, but accepted that there was not enough time to make major changes. 'It is too late at this stage to suggest alternative methods . . . which could occupy less space in a ship and take less time in the process.' In thanking him for his report, Colonel Newbold, the Chairman of the Brewers' Society, revealed his fears:

'I may tell you privately that I have been very worried about these ships because of course the Admiralty and Adlams dashed into the matter without consultation with the Brewers' Society . . . and as you emphasise in your report, it is too late now to make any major alterations. Further, even today as far as I know no-one has detailed plans of the plant!'

The floating breweries were all at sea – and sailing further and further behind schedule. In January the breweries were expected to be ready by June. By July a memo was talking hopefully about the first brew going through on 10 October.

The brewing materials themselves did not present too many problems, though the scale of the order did strain the suppliers. By the summer of 1945, 500 tons of malt extract had been ordered from eight different manufacturers, with two-thirds of it having been made and a quarter delivered to the Admiralty. The difficulty was in the containers.

It had originally been planned to use hundredweight drums with tin plate linings, but it proved impossible to obtain these in time. The only drums of that size available were either made out of black steel, which might taint the extract, or lined with plate containing lead, which could have contaminated the beer. Eventually 70lb tin plate drums which usually contained paint had to be used, though they were far from ideal. Lance McMullen admitted that they were really 'of insufficient strength for a valuable and potentially explosive substance like malt extract.'

The hop concentrate proved less troublesome. Some 3,500lbs were supplied by White, Tomkins & Courage from Reigate in Surrey.

Two Blue Funnel liners, *Agamemnon* and *Menestheus*, which had been used to lay mines, were sent to Canada to be fitted out with the breweries shipped from Bristol and a wide variety of other amenities including a theatre, cinema, restaurant and shops. However the plans were overtaken by events. On 6 August the Americans dropped the first atomic bomb on Japan at Hiroshima. On 9 August the second fell on Nagasaki. On 14 August the Japanese surrendered. The war which had been expected to last another 18 months after victory in Europe, had folded in three months.

The floating breweries were left high and dry. The plans for a land-based brewery were immediately called off and a contract for 100 tons of malt extract which had not yet been made was cancelled. But Lance McMullen did set out for Canada the day after victory over Japan was formally celebrated on 2 September. There were still vast forces in the Far East and they deserved something to toast the final success.

However, with the end of the war, the urgency had been drained from the scheme, as Lance McMullen reported:

Early in September the head brewers of the two amenity ships and I proceeded to Vancouver. While we were on the way the completion dates of both ships were put back a month, and it

FULL STEAM AHEAD: The *Menestheus* at sea. The forward stack was the brewery chimney. After refitting at Hebburn in 1946, the cargo ship was lost in a fire off California in 1953.

soon became clear that even the new dates were pious hopes. The whole work of conversion had turned out to be a far bigger job than had been expected, and one of the shipyards concerned was lacking in the technical skill, the organisation and the will to perform the unprecedented task of installing a brewery in a ship.

Progress was painfully slow, punctuated by setbacks and aggravated by the non-arrival of brewery parts from England. In November it was decided to abandon plans to equip the *Agamemnon* and to concentrate on the *Menestheus*. Meanwhile Guinness's yeast was struggling to survive the delays, and was only kept alive thanks to the help of the agriculture department at the University of British Columbia.

Eventually the first test brew, with several improvisations, was carried out on 31 December, 1945, with a second put through a week later on 7 January. 'The beer made in the trial brews was immediately popular and was sold at the commissioning parties and later in Tokyo Bay as late as 15 March, 1946,' said head brewer George Brown, who had been head brewer at Truman's London brewery before the war, and had been specially brought back from service with the London Scottish in Italy to take charge of the plant.

Along with his assistant brewer, Ken Morrison from Hancock's Brewery in Cardiff, he called the new plant Davy Jones' Brewery. Just one beer was produced, an 'English Mild Ale' with a gravity of 1037, though Ken Morrison described it 'as rather akin to a London

Mild and Bitter.' It was promoted as 'something from the old country' and 'a breath from Britain.' The aim had been to provide homesick troops with a nostalgic taste of home. Yet the beer barely got through to Britain's war-weary soldiers.

The brewery had been supplied with some 1,200 five-gallon containers for supplying mess rooms and other forces' bars, but much to head brewer George Brown's disgust little attempt was made to sell the beer beyond the ship itself. *Menestheus*'s first ports of call were Yokohama and Kure in Japan and Shanghai in China, where overside sales were small.

BREWING BELOW: Part of the plant in the hold. Brewing was carried out by dissolving one ton of malt extract with distilled water from the hot liquor tank (left) in the large dissolving tank (centre) behind the wooden platform. This was boiled in the 55-barrel pressure copper (right) and circulated through a small cylinder holding a 7lb pierced tin of hop concentrate. After cooling through a paraflow heat exchanger using sea water, the wort was aerated and pumped into one of six 50-barrel pressure fermenters. These squat steel vessels, insulated with brine jackets and six inches of cork, were completely enclosed except for swan-neck pipes rising to yeast backs on the deck above. Once pitched with 30lbs of yeast, the wort was left to ferment for six days and then cooled, carbonated, fined and allowed to settle for two days. The beer was then filtered into a bright beer tank from where it could be served direct to the bar or filled into five-gallon drums.

'Despite the verbal statement made to me in the early discussions that ratings in non-fighting ships would be allowed to purchase this beer through their messes or canteen manager, no dispensations had been made by Fleet Order to permit this,' reported George Brown. 'To me it seemed strange that so elaborate and expensive measures should have been taken to produce beer, and yet so limit the opportunity of 90 per cent of the potential customers to consume the product.'

The main outlet for the beer was therefore the ship's own bar where the fined and filtered ale was served under pressure through ten taps direct from bright beer storage tanks. To add to its attraction the beer passed through observation glasses and was sold at 9d a pint. Yet even here availability was limited, the bar only opening from 6pm to 10pm when in port and for two of those four hours visitors were usually in the theatre. 'The petty officer in charge of the bar in addition took every opportunity to put the shutters up,' reported a frustrated George Brown.

> Only in enterprising Hong Kong was the brewery really busy: We were alongside a wharf and ratings from other ships could purchase beer and set up a canteen on the breakwater near their own ship. There were also many ratings and royal marines in barracks in the dockyard with canteen and mess facilities. And there was the China Fleet Club, the officials of which displayed enterprise, being on the ship immediately on arrival and arranging for the supply of beer, averaging 400 gallons daily.

Many eminent men were shown round the unique installation including Lord Louis Mountbatten, Britain's supreme commander in South-East Asia, and the Admiral of the British Pacific Fleet, Lord Fraser. All were impressed. Visiting American admirals were envious. Yet, with the war ended, the Admiralty and the NAAFI had lost interest in their new toy. The *Menestheus* was ordered back to Britain.

On the journey home the little-used amenity ship called in at Saletar (Singapore) for one day, Trincomalee (Ceylon) for three days, Aden for one day, Malta for three days and Gibraltar for one day. Again George Brown reported that no effort was made to sell what was still a rare and rationed product. The Admiralty just wanted to forget the whole project. The *Menestheus* was directed from Portsmouth to the Tyne to have the brewery removed and to be refitted as a fast cargo liner. A huge stock of malt extract was left for disposal.

THE ROYAL NAVY AMENITY SHIP
"MENESTHEUS"

~ BEER ~

ENGLISH MILD ALE

Brewed in

Davy Jones Brewery

"THE WORLD'S ONLY
FLOATING BREWERY"

On Sale at all BARS of the AMENITY SHIP
9d per Pint   SUPPLIES UNLIMITED

Operated By

NAVY, ARMY & AIR FORCE INSTITUTES
SPONSORED BY BOARD OF ADMIRALTY

DAVY JONES' DELIGHT:
A poster advertising the
special brew. Altogether
over a quarter of a million
pints were sold in six
months.

The brewery had been in operation for less than six months. The chairman of the 'Beer for Troops' Committee, Mr F A Simonds, commented in a letter to the new chairman of the Brewers' Society, Commander Redmond McGrath, on 4 July, 1946: 'I should imagine that a great deal of money has been wasted and a lot of trouble taken unnecessarily over this venture.'

His words were true but failed to pay tribute to a remarkable achievement. The brewery had been a technical success against tremendous odds. Early problems with too much yeast left in the fermenting tanks, resulting in high beer losses of 11 per cent, had been overcome.

Even the beer's odd tang quickly became a selling point. A visitor who said after finishing a glass that while it was 'a pleasant drink, its malt extract origin could be detected' was told that 'the flavour so grew on one that one soon swore by this brew above all others.'

But the project suffered from the fallout from the two atomic bombs which brought the war with Japan to a sudden end. Its whole purpose had been blown away months before the first pint poured out of Davy Jones' locker.

BREWING UNDER THE JACKBOOT
The Channel Islands – and Beyond

One part of the British Isles was captured by the Germans. In June 1940 the Government decided not to defend the Channel Islands, evacuating a substantial part of the population. Those who were left behind faced five years of fear and deprivation.

But for one brewery these long, lean years became a test of ingenuity and a battle of wits against the occupying forces. The Guernsey Brewery of St Peter Port lost most of its directors and many of its workers in the evacuation, but fortunately its head brewer Roy Higgs had decided to stay. 'He proved to be a tower of strength,' recalled secretary Mr D A Bourgaize. 'He took the occupation as a challenge and devoted his energies to experimenting in various ways to produce substitute beers. It was often said that Roy could produce a silk purse out of a sow's ear.' It was a skill that was to be tested again and again in the months ahead.

At the start of the occupation the harbour-side Guernsey Brewery

LOST PONY: The Guernsey Brewery's popular Pony Ales soon vanished during the war as malt supplies ran out to be replaced by a variety of ingenious substitute beers.

had good stocks of sugar and hops and a limited amount of malt. The nearby Vauxlaurens Brewery of R W Randall was not so fortunate and soon had to close. Its bottling plant was commandeered by the Germans and its chairman, Lt Colonel R W Randall, who had served with the Royal Guernsey Militia, was later interned with his family in Germany.

To conserve stocks, the Guernsey Brewery reduced the gravities of its 'Pony Ales' (as they were known after the polo-playing founder of the company) and rationed supplies. Some beer was also delivered to Randall's for their pubs. An early crisis threatened when the authorities tried to requisition part of the brewery's malt stock. The bakers had run out of yeast for making bread and were instructed to use brewer's yeast. The malt was needed to provide a continuous supply of yeast, but Roy Higgs averted the danger by producing a better baker's barm from invert sugar.

One problem could not be avoided. Petrol was severely restricted and the company's lorries were taken over by the Germans. Alternative transport had to be found. At first horses cantered to the rescue of Pony Ales, but then these were also commandeered. The company was reduced to using men pulling and pushing carts. 'Hard work on meagre rations in hilly St Peter Port,' recalled Mr Bourgaize. What was a struggle for local deliveries, was no use at all for longer hauls. So the brewery hitched its wagon – to a bull.

BULL POWER: The docile bull which delivered to Guernsey Brewery's pubs during the war.

The bull was a centre of attraction and amusement, a diversion much needed in those grim days. It was, of course, led by its keeper and performed its task with docility, rather suggestive that it was past its prime for breeding or perhaps, like so many humans at the time, it was suffering from occupation lethargy.

One individual who was far from lethargic was Roy Higgs, who had joined the Guernsey Brewery from his father's Lion Brewery in Reading in 1936. He was determined to keep the brewery going. 'Closure was viewed as Doomsday.' It was quickly apparent that the company's limited stock of malt would run out by October 1940, so the Germans were asked for a supply from France since many of their troops were drinking the beer. They refused. Roy Higgs responded by producing brews from invert sugar and hops only, which were at first blended with the regular mild and stout. When the malt stocks were exhausted, this special 'process beer' became their sole ale.

'To be quite frank, the public was not enthusiastic with this process beer,' admitted Mr Bourgaize. 'It was passable during the summer months, but it could not be classed as a winter drink.' So Roy Higgs reached back into the recipe book – and came up with porter. This was produced using a similar brew of invert sugar and hops, but with added caramel to give the beer more body and flavour. Being a black beer, it also did not need fining to make it clear.

This porter was well received at the bar, but soon the brewery was running out of invert sugar and caramel. This was replaced in 1941 by supplies of sugar beet and unmalted barley from France, which were used to make a bottled light ale. However, in April 1941, the Germans tried to slam the lid on the mash tun by ordering that further supplies of sugar for brewing were prohibited. Fortunately, the brewery had built up a good stock and this continued to be used sparingly. The Germans also unwittingly came to the brewery's rescue.

On August bank holiday 1941 the Germans brought a large consignment of German and French beer to the island and the casks were stored at the brewery. When a further huge load of 3,000 casks arrived from Dortmund the following week, many were stacked outside in the summer sun. Much of the beer was rapidly going sour, having been long in transit.

Roy Higgs saw his opportunity. There were 50,000 gallons of beer stored in and around the brewery, far in excess of the needs of the German troops. He offered to buy it. He suggested that if he was allowed to purchase the sour beer at a low price, along with half a ton of sugar and two tons of coal, he could recondition it. He pointed out that the alternative was to pour most of it down the drain. The Germans agreed but wanted all the reconditioned beer for themselves. Roy Higgs rejected this and, after much haggling, it was agreed to split the beer 50:50 between the islanders and the troops. The brewery did well out of this deal. Much of the reconditioned beer was blended with their own beer, camouflaged from the authorities by darkening it with caramel and sold as Dark Ale. 'The German troops said it was very good, greatly to our financial advantage and secret amusement,' said war-time director George Burlingham.

The company also gained a smile of satisfaction when the Germans requisitioned the brewery board room and other offices in March 1942. The order mentioned nothing about furniture, so the tables and chairs were removed, the carpets rolled up and the curtains packed away. The incoming Nazi officers were not amused.

The German beer had provided a useful bonus, but the hard reality was that the company's sugar supplies were almost spent. Roy Higgs kept the pubs happy by buying up grape juice and converting it at the brewery into port-like 'Sarnia Wine' until supplies of grape juice ran out. Then country wines were attempted using parsnips, but without the same success. Some cider was also obtained from Normandy.

Eventually, with all sugar gone, Roy Higgs turned early in 1942 to the production of non-alcoholic hop bitters, using by now very old hops, saccharine and a little grain spirit provided by local wine merchants Bucktrout. This thin Hop Ale sold well as a summer refresher, but was not so popular in colder weather. So he tried adding the residue of the parsnips left over from the unsuccessful country wine. This much improved the ale, giving the brew a foaming head. Many publicans got round the fact that it was non-alcoholic by selling it half-and-half with cider to make a pleasant drink.

On 15 September, 1942, the brewery was dealt a crushing blow when the Germans ordered that all persons living in the Channel Islands aged 16-70, but born in the United Kingdom, must be deported to prison camps in Germany. This cruel net caught not only two brewery directors but also the resourceful brewer Roy Higgs and his right hand man, brewing foreman Jim Scrivens.

Before he was taken away, Roy Higgs passed on the recipe for Hop Ale to the secretary, Mr Bourgaize, who was left in charge. He ensured production continued at the rate of 40 barrels a week, with Jim Scrivens' assistant Arthur Snaith acting as brewer. With the curfew closing pubs at 8.30pm, this proved adequate for the diminished population, along with supplies of cider and the occasional windfall of German beer.

Brewing was maintained despite part of the brewery being turned into a military hospital, with large red crosses painted on the roof and walls. The general office was converted into an operating theatre and a mortuary slab was built in the garage. This was constructed out of reinforced concrete, the same material that was being used by armies of slave labour round the island to build massive defence works. The secretary expressed surprise at the solid structure. 'I don't know why reinforced concrete was used – dead men don't struggle.' After the war, it proved almost impossible to shift.

These were grim days, as Mr Bourgaize recalled. 'I remember on more than one occasion arriving at the brewery to be confronted by blood-stained stretchers lined up against the front of the premises prior to being washed down. This was sometimes following naval actions at sea, of which there were quite a few, and also after Allied aerial attacks on military objects in the island.' Equally harrowing, a building behind the brewery was used as a prison. 'From time to time prisoners were physically punished and their screams could be heard in the brewery.'

When the Allied forces hit the Normandy beaches, there were huge sighs of relief and stifled cheers. But hopes of a quick liberation were soon dashed. The Allied armies headed for Berlin and the Channel Islands had to wait until the end of the war for their freedom.

Meanwhile the non-alcoholic Hop Ale was going from strength to strength, despite dropping the use of parsnips as the new vegetable crop tended to leave 'a strong taste of the root which it was difficult to eradicate.' Instead, it was learnt from experience that long storage of the ale, much improved the drink. Islanders were developing a strong liking for the weak brew. Early in 1944 sales increased twentyfold, as wine and cider supplies ran low. 'This sudden swing in favour of Hop Ale was a pleasurable surprise,' recorded Mr Bourgaize.

There were instances on record of quite a few individual licensees reporting to the brewery the liking which their customers had acquired for the product. One in particular cycled to the brewery asking if he could buy some of the NEW beer. The manager of St Saviour's Hotel came along saying that his customers had asked if they could have some of the

UNDER ATTACK: The waterfront brewhouse had its windows repeatedly blown out, first by German bombers in 1940 and then by the RAF. These buildings at the southern end of the Esplanade were completely rebuilt in 1948.

IMPORTED beer on sale in the town. The driver of Messrs R W Randall remarked on the sudden rush for Hop Ale, stating that he had seen beer at Grandes Rocques Hotel with an excellent head on it and instanced much stronger stuff being turned down for Hop Ale. He had seen six pints of beer lined up on the counter with a nice creamy head – a really fine sight in those hard-off days.

Mr Bourgaize attributed the new popularity to increased carbonation and the fact that Arthur Snaith had been 'turning it out in a light colour with just the correct sweetness and, being nice and bright, it looked very much like lager and had a pleasant flavour.' Sadly, Arthur Snaith developed tuberculosis and eventually died, his place as brewer being taken by engineer Eric Chapple.

Following the D-Day landings the German-occupied islands were under siege with their supply lines cut. The occupation had begun with German bombs in the harbour blowing out the windows in the waterfront brewery. It ended in the same way, only this time the bombs belonged to the RAF. Havelet Bay became a battlefront, with the brewery having repeatedly to close as the building was shaken again and again by blasts.

Mr Bourgaize brought an old heavy door bell from home to provide warning of Allied air-raids. It was an exhausting business:

> On hearing the siren or aircraft, I quickly ran from my office up a flight of stairs to and through the bottle store, out into the yard and down the stairs to the cellars, all the time clanging the bell as an alarm.

Supplies were now at crisis level. The only saccharine which could be obtained was in weaker tablet rather than powdered form. Fuel was in such short supply that tree stumps were dragged in and yard sweepings mixed with tar to keep the furnace going. The reduced boil and poorer brewing materials meant that the Hop Ale often became unstable. The electricity supply was cut forcing Eric Chapple to introduce many manual improvisations like a handle on the bottle rinsing machine. A new age of darkness descended. Pubs were only allowed to use 1½ units of electricity a week over the normal household allowance. This amounted to one 40-watt bulb for 30 hours a week. The last straw came when the Germans stopped water supplies to the brewery, a reprieve only being granted at the last minute on the understanding that all cask and bottle washing be carried out using rain water collected in a large cistern.

A small brew was put through at the end of April 1945. It was to be the last of the occupation. Liberation came on 8 May with the announcement that the war was over. Mr Bourgaize recalled:

> That afternoon the staff and employees gathered in the workshop where an illicitly stored wireless set, now resuscitated, was connected to the mains to hear Winston Churchill's historic broadcast, including the words "Our dear Channel Islands are to be freed today".

No more Hop Ale was brewed and what was in the pubs was recalled. The brewery felt it was better to have no beer at all, rather than serve the liberating troops with ersatz beer. The thirsty British forces quickly ensured that supplies of malt and hops and other vital materials were obtained and the pubs reopened with proper Pony Ales on Saturday, 4 August, 1945. The five-year nightmare was over.

Randall's nearby Vauxlaurens Brewery bounced back into production once the returning family had managed to coax the disused and neglected plant into operation. Fortunately German plans to remove most of the equipment had never been put into effect. On Jersey, the Anne Street Brewery also started brewing again.

At least the Channel Islands breweries did not suffer the fate of the famous Tuborg Brewery in Copenhagen, which was blown up by the Germans in January 1945 as an act of revenge and retaliation against the resistance of the Danish nation.

Another substantial number of British people under the heel of the German jackboot were prisoners-of-war. Even here, inside the barbed wire camps, beer helped raise morale – or at least talking about the tantalising drop had that effect.

Lieutenant J R Lawrence had been captured at Dunkirk and sent to a prison camp in Germany. In August 1940 he gave a lecture on brewing to a captive audience of 800:

> creating so much interest that during the next three months
> weekly talks were given around the cells. We had the help of
> a Norfolk barley farmer, a merchant, three brewers, an excise
> officer and a publican, so that our lectures were under-
> standably among the most popular.

Gradually the talks became more serious. After being moved to Oflag V1B in Westphalia at the end of 1941, a proper brewing school was established with the assistance of Colonel John Courage and other captured brewery directors. The normal college comforts were missing:

> Classrooms in this dirty, ill-lighted camp were lacking, so we
> had to gather at the end of the soup hut during the hours of
> darkness and hold our discussions around a little acetylene
> lamp. More often than not we listened in complete darkness.
> Nevertheless, we could usually muster about 15 brewers,
> directors and allied traders.

Managing to contact the Bodleian Library at Oxford, the group began more intensive studies for the Institute of Brewing examination. 'We considered that work with a tangible end in view would take a man's mind off the everyday monotony of camp life.' Two officers, one a brewer and the other a director, were eligible to sit Part II of the Institute exams. Both passed with honours, gaining 82 and 79 per cent. The success spurred more to have a go, some taking the City and Guilds paper, one winning the Silver Medal. It was no mean achievement. It was not easy for students to concentrate in the packed prison camp holding 4,000 – until some found an ideal quiet spot.

> Several officers studying for examinations, and unable to get
> peace in their own huts, changed over with others who were
> due to serve sentences in the cells. There they would be in

absolute solitude which suited them perfectly. The Germans were none the wiser provided the prisoner wore the appropriate identification disc.

The brewing class widened its interests and with the help of some solicitors organised a full-scale mock Brewster Licensing Session with proper court procedures. As the war progressed they even began to look forward to a future beyond the barbed wire.

Our study circle became so well-known around the camp that a number of qualified and unqualified architects joined us for discussions upon post-war rebuilding problems for public houses. Given hypothetical sites and the directors' instructions regarding types and costs, their finished plans were criticised by the school. This work served them in good stead, for when the first set of architectural examination papers arrived from England one of the RIBA requirements was a complete set of plans for a post-war workmen's pub.

In the last year this remarkable brewing school saw six candidates sit and pass with distinction the City and Guilds paper, while another two were successful in Part I of the Institute of Brewing examination.

Lieutenant Lawrence was due to read a paper on his war-time experiences before the London and South of England Incorporated Brewers' Guild in November 1945. But before he could attend the meeting, he suffered a relapse of an illness contracted in the prison camp and died within a few weeks. His paper was read by a fellow POW, Captain D L Flower.

THE PINT IN PEACE
The Pub after the War

The Second World War settled two scores. During the 1930s, Hitler had schemed and screamed in Europe, while prohibition had threatened to spread from the United States. The war routed them both, preventing either gaining a foothold in Britain.

The *Brewing Trade Review* could confidently reflect as early as May 1943: 'The war has broken up many old prejudices and dispelled many deep-rooted illusions. None, perhaps, has been more completely shattered than the idea that the devil lurks at the bottom of every glass of beer.'

The conflict set the seal on the trend towards lighter, weaker beers introduced in the First World War and continued between the wars. 'In pre-1914 days beer was largely drunk for the kick in it,' said *The Brewers' Journal* in July 1942. 'Brewers would then tell you that the public were able to detect a two degrees alteration in the gravity of

MILD SETBACK: Mild was the most popular drink before the war, but the conflict weakened its character and loosened its stranglehold. Some specialist bottled beers also vanished. (*Western Mail*).

mild ale, and would patronise the houses that sold the heavier gravity beer.'

Alcoholic punch had long since ceased to be the key issue. But drinkers still sought quality. Before 1939 the vast bulk of beer enjoyed in Britain had been draught mild ale at 5d a pint – a cheap but satisfying drink. This tasty bread-and-butter brew never fully regained its popularity after the war. During the conflict it lost much of its character and once regular supplies of other beers were eventually restored, many younger drinkers turned to the sharper tastes of bitter, a beer little in demand before 1939 in comparison to mild.

The sales of more reliable bottled beers also began to sparkle, supported by advertising campaigns behind strong brand names. Image was to become much more important than intoxication.

At the same time the wide variety of beers once brewed dwindled. 'Before the war every palate and purse were catered for,' commented *The Brewers' Journal* in September 1943.

A wide range of draught and bottled beers were produced by the average brewery, from thirst-quenching, low-gravity harvest beers to high-grade ales. Even in similar beers such as mild ales there were sometimes provided a light mild ale and a dark mild ale to cater for the eye and palate. Special beers were brewed for the family trade, mainly luncheon and dinner ales for consumption in the home. Golden ale, brown ale, nut brown ale and stouts in a large variety were produced to maintain or capture trade or because a rival brewer had created a demand by brewing a new type of beer.

This rich range of colours, gravities and styles had been decimated by the war and never fully recovered. Many had been low-selling speciality brews which some companies were happy to dispense with, while the high duty rates – which were not only maintained but increased after the war – ensured that few of the heavier beers bounced back.

The writer of the *Journal*'s bottling notes lamented in January 1945: 'It seems years since the cheering order "A nip of barley wine, please," has been given. Today there is no barley wine and no nip-size bottles; the former is not brewed and the latter is not made.'

The Brewers' Journal in January 1944 even urged the industry to promote beer 'as a temperance drink' because its weak strength meant that it was a 'relatively non-intoxicating product.' This could be pushed too far. That same month the *Daily Express* ran an interview with the managing director of a well-known brewery under the headline 'I cannot think why people go on drinking beer.' Ale's reputation was not helped by the former Minister of Food, Lord Woolton, cheekily telling the House of Lords that 'the greater barrel-age of beer now being drunk consists largely of water – a beverage which is approved by the highest authorities.'

Yet the public lapped it up. Some said demand had increased because drinkers needed to down more pints to become merry, at a time when wines and spirits were scarce. The reality was that despite testing war-time conditions, British beer was still a decent drop of cheer in a mean and dangerous world.

'When the whole story of brewing in wartime can be told, the men who will rank for very high praise are the operative brewers of Britain who, surmounting difficulties which their predecessors would have regarded as insuperable, give the public beers as good as they are today,' commented *The Brewers' Journal* in June 1944. Instead of decrying beer's weakness, said the magazine, everyone should be thankful 'that in this war the public has been able to obtain vastly more of it than in the last.'

The columnist 'Brettanomyces' concluded in May 1945:

Although the gravity of beer has progressively declined during the war, the quality and drinkability of the extremely light beers which have constituted the bulk of the beverage of the country have been higher than one could have dared to hope.

The brewers had feared that these weak brews with their low hopping rates would rapidly turn sour. This danger had been averted by the heavy demand at the bar. 'In other words, the beer has scarcely had time to go off.'

As the war lurched to a close, there were calls for stronger beer. Reading Licensed Victuallers' Association passed a resolution in March 1945 urging the local Berkshire Brewers' Union 'in accordance with insistent public demand for stronger beer, to consider carefully the possibility of supplying a higher proportion of heavier beer.' This demand was to be denied, as restrictions and rationing intensified in the immediate post-war years.

While many raised their glasses to beer's enduring popularity, the pub had risen even higher in public esteem. It was no longer just a place to have a drink, but the very heart of the community. Its place in the affections of the people was secure – but its future shape was wide open to debate.

Welcome
to the Inn

beer is best

PUB FIRST: After the war the Brewers' Society switched the emphasis of its 'Beer is Best' campaign to promoting the warm welcome of the inn, with women now firmly in the bar.

Between the wars a number of leading brewers like Whitbread and Watney's in London and Mitchell's & Butler's in Birmingham had been building 'bigger and better' houses. Prompted and pushed by licensing benches bent on reform, the idea had been to replace a number of small, shady, street-corner pubs with one large, bright, road house with much wider facilities. Architects' journals were full of hope for the new 'improved' pubs. Government ministers and town councillors praised them.

With many city pubs damaged or destroyed during the war, the reformers believed the German bombers had cleared the way for more widespread action. Thomas Cox, chairman of the Newington Licensing Bench in London declared early in 1941: 'A comprehensive scheme should be launched whereby brewers, owners and others would pool their resources and co-operate in replacing a number of licensed houses in one thoroughfare by one up-to-date house with every amenity for the public.' Snugs and small bars should be replaced by open expanses of tables and comfortable chairs. The gloom of Dickensian dens should be swept away by modern designs of good taste. The *Brewing Trade Review* of September 1941 revealed the new vision of replacing 'old and unworthy premises' with much more suitable buildings:

Many an old Victorian public house has disappeared from the street corner and its lurid gaslight will no longer be seen streaming through the ornately frosted windows and reflecting from the wet pavement. . . . The cab horse has gone, the cobble stones have given place to tarmac, and our bewhiskered grandfathers might well be forgiven if they had mistaken that tasteful building set back a little from the corner of the road for a museum or one of those newly founded Carnegie free libraries, until that little legend on the door has led them into the bar where the Englishman and his friends foregather to enjoy their refreshment in comfortable chairs with a little table on which to rest their glasses, the bar counter fulfilling its real purpose as the place for serving drinks and freed from its erstwhile duty of supporting the elbows of the entire clientele.

There was just one problem. The public was not so impressed with these impersonal palaces. They preferred their local. And in the people's war, the people's voice could no longer be ignored. The pubs now belonged to them just as much as the brewers and the licensing authorities.

Sir Francis Lindley, the chairman of Meux's Brewery of London, told his AGM in 1941:

Our future policy is to rebuild our damaged properties on the same lines – with improvements if such be called for – as those destroyed. We are against the idea supported in some quarters of the erection of a few large houses to replace a number of small ones. The public prefer small houses, and it is our business to cater for what the public want, and not for what some think they ought to want.

Even *The Brewers' Journal*, long an advocate of change, recognised that 'the vast proportion of customers of licensed houses dislike bigness.' People preferred 'friendly little houses of distinction and character' rather than what it termed 'standardised tea-shops' or places with all the atmosphere of a central post office.

This sharp swing in attitude was partly because many brewers had begun to feel confident and secure enough to stand up for the traditional pub. Now that the temperance movement had been routed, those tinkering with the future of what had become a national institution could be challenged.

The change was also because many customers had already talked with their pockets. The social engineers could not make people drink in their sterile schemes. The huge new houses, with their high overheads and large staff, had failed to bring in the expected profits.

The Brewers' Journal admitted in July 1941:

Brewers are already regretting the outsize type of houses which they have erected. One such house we have in mind has an acre of licensed space, excluding gardens. Such an experiment is not likely to be repeated. True, its opening was regarded as of sufficient news value to occupy considerable space in the daily press. But that may have proved small compensation for the immense standing charges for light, heating and upkeep, not to mention staff difficulties.

More than all else the factors that are likely to militate against the multiplication of really large public houses are two-fold: they do not pay and the public does not like them.

Two years later the magazine concluded:

The palatial over-large licensed house has performed its purpose in showing the way to development for the future. But there is now clear evidence that improvement must not be judged in terms of size so much as in terms of intimacy and character.

It was not just the oversize pub which was rapidly falling out of favour. So were the houses which tried to pretend they were anything but a pub, as *The Brewers' Journal* predicted in November 1941:

Nor will prevail – if brewers have their way – the immediate pre-war tendency to build, as one critic put it, a series of lavatories with one or two bars attached. We refer to the kind of public house so beloved and belauded by some licensing benches consisting of one or more luncheon rooms, a children's room, a tea room, separate lavatories for both sexes adjacent to each bar, a games room and a garden. As one irate customer said after wandering fruitlessly around such a masonic mass for some time, 'Where's the pub?' This type of new licensed house, as we see now looking back in retrospect, was reform gone crazy.

No-one expected the pub to stand still. But it should evolve rather than change overnight, losing all its character in an antiseptic onslaught. Food, for instance, should be introduced but not huge dining rooms. In this, the new mood was helped by war-time and post-war restrictions; it was almost impossible to gain permission for major building works.

The emphasis changed from altering the physical layout of the pub to raising its social status further through activities which brewers would once never have dreamed about in the bar. **The Fish Inn** at Wixford in Warwickshire, for instance, held a Pub Brains' Trust in 1943 in which four parsons discussed religious and social issues with the regulars. **The Red Lion** at Cerne Abbas in Dorset developed a debating club. **The Freemasons' Arms** in Hampstead established a Pub Parliament in 1942, meeting every Friday to discuss issues of the day from 'Why France Fell' to 'The Future of Philosophy.'

The Brewers' Journal proposed in June 1943 that pubs should put on plays, poetry readings and exhibitions; newspapers and a book exchange could be provided in areas without a lending library. 'There is every reason to suppose that in the post-war period this emphasis on the cultural character of the pub will be accelerated.'

Some brewers swallowed the advice. In London in 1944 four prominent companies – Barclay, Courage, Watney and Whitbread – financed a movement commissioning artists to paint pictures to hang in pubs. In October 1945 the resulting works were exhibited at the Suffolk Street Gallery off Pall Mall after a grand lunch at the **Savoy** attended by members of the Government. The 165 pictures, many by famous artists, were then distributed in batches round London bars. The first pub display was unveiled by Augustus John at **The Cogers** in Salisbury Court off Fleet Street. Augustus John said artists had always been staunch supporters of the brewing industry and were pleased by this reciprocal action.

In Yorkshire Tennant's of Sheffield in 1944 embarked on an equally ambitious scheme. After consulting Malcolm Sargent, the brewery decided to put on classical concerts at suitable pubs featuring top musicians. Nine of their larger houses in the steel city, plus others in

ALE AND ARTY: Painter, Augustus John, admires one of the landscapes at the opening of the first pub art display at **The Cogers** near Fleet Street.

Rotherham and Doncaster, were involved. The inaugural concert featuring oboist Leon Goossens was held at **The Brincliffe Oaks** on 4 September. The Lord Mayor of Sheffield in opening the recital described the idea as 'very bold, very daring and very commendable.' The Polish bass Nowakowski sang to 400 people at **The Wharncliffe**. A few complained that the waiters stopped serving pints during the performance, but otherwise the music went down well. Tennant's managing director Captain M H Francis said that the first series of 20 concerts had been 'an unqualified success' reaching 7,500 customers. A second, longer series followed early in 1945, spreading to the Midlands after Tennant's takeover of the Nottingham Brewery. Some recitals were in small houses, pianist Mark Hambourg performing in a pub in the mining village of South Elmsall. *The Times* applauded the initiative, declaring that the tavern was 'staking out a claim to be considered a centre of civilised social life.'

Such schemes were rare but demonstrated the new standing and aspirations of the pub. It had never been so popular. There was one major worry for the brewers as the war ground to a halt – the aspirations of the new Labour Government which had been elected in July 1945.

One of its leading figures, Herbert Morrison, while Home Secretary in the War Cabinet, had visited Carlisle in 1941. He had sampled the state beer, played bowls at one of the state pubs and been impressed. Asked about a possible extension of state control, he then replied: 'This scheme has been eminently successful, and the moral is pretty clear.'

Now Labour was in power on its own, the brewers sweated over

NEW ENEMY: Brewers feared that the new Labour Government might nationalise the brewing industry. This cartoon was produced by Groves & Whitnall of Salford.

VICTORY ALE: Greenall Whitley's special brew celebrated not only the end of the war but also the enhanced stature of beer and the pub. The temperance movement had been completely routed by 1945.

their beer glasses. Nationalisation embraced everything from the coal mines and the railways to the Bank of England. Would the licensed trade follow? Leicester Corporation had already proposed in 1944 that it would run any new pubs built on its new housing estates.

But the protection of the brewing industry lay in the high regard in which the pub was held. There was not enough pressure for change of ownership at a time when the Labour Government was wrestling with major developments like the establishment of the National Health Service and the nationalisation of the steel industry.

The trade could shelter behind the bar from the strong winds of change blowing through the land. The glow of the war-time welcome lingered long. The pub had been widely praised by visiting troops. Whitbread's **Central Hotel** in Hastings was even renamed **The GI** in December 1945 in honour of the American servicemen.

The Agent-General for Ontario wrote after the war:

Hundreds of thousands of Canadians have grown to love your people and your mode of life, and they have largely made the discovery through the medium of your village inns.

Each one should be decorated for its magnificent war service in creating friendliness and mutual understanding, in addition to its pleasant task of dispensing hospitality. Our returning boys say 'God bless the British licensed house.' It saved our lives from loneliness; it is a glorious institution, and may it live and prosper for ever.

VICTORY: A wagon load of beer passing through Piccadilly Circus on VE- Day. The expressions of some of the men sitting on top suggest they have tasted a drop.

BIBLIOGRAPHY

Those wanting further information on the history of the brewing industry should consult:

The British Brewing Industry 1830-1980, T R Gourvish and R G Wilson, Cambridge University Press, 1994.

Those seeking further information on the pub need look no further than:

The English Pub, A History, Peter Haydon, Robert Hale, 1994.

Individual brewery histories which detail the war period include:

A Brewer's Progress (Charrington), L A G Strong, 1957.
History of the Brewery (Groves & Whitnall), 1835-1949, Manchester, 1949.
Guinness Book of Guinness, 1935-1985, Edward Guinness, Enfield, 1988.
Story of Watneys, W P Serocold, 1949.

INDEX